Flowers, the Angels' Alphabet

Flowers, the Angels' Alphabet

The Language and Poetry of Flowers

WITH
AN AMERICAN FLORAL DICTIONARY
AND
TWENTY-EIGHT LITERARY CALLIGRAPHY® ILLUSTRATIONS

Susan Loy

CSL Press

Book design by Susan Loy
Jacket design by Susan Loy and Ron Ayers

CSL Press
Moneta, Virginia 24121

First Edition
Published 2001

9 8 7 6 5 4 3 2 1

Library of Congress Card Catalog Number: 00-111571

Library of Congress Cataloging-in-Publication Data
Loy, Susan.
        Flowers, the angels' alphabet : the language and
    poetry of flowers ; with, an American floral dictionary
    and twenty-eight literary calligraphy illustrations /
    Susan Loy. -- 1st ed.
        p. cm.
        Includes bibliographical references and index.
        ISBN 0-9702113-1-7

    1. Flowers. 2. Flowers--Folklore. 3. Flowers--
    Dictionaries. 4. Flowers in art. 5. Calligraphy.
    6. Gardening. I. Title.

    SB405.L69 2001   635.9
                       QB100-902080

Printed in the United States of America

Flowers are the alphabet of angels, – whereby
They write on hills and fields mysterious truths.
John Stowell Adams, *Flora's Album*

CONTENTS

CONTENTS

ILLUSTRATIONS

All illustrations are reproductions of original Literary Calligraphy® watercolor paintings by Susan Loy.

ACKNOWLEDGEMENTS

To R. Tapp, my editor and friend, whose assistance has been invaluable, I send a moss rose, an emblem of superior merit.

To Ron Ayers, my partner in marriage, business, and dance, for his help on this book and in all ways, I send honeysuckle, an emblem of my devoted love.

To Ellen Knauer for her assistance with the French translation of Charlotte de Latour's *Le Langage Des Fleurs*, I send a crested iris, an emblem of my compliments.

To Beverly Seaton for her book, *The Language of Flowers: A History,* I send meadowsweet, an emblem of praise.

To Tara Azwell, Mary Anne Garbowsky, Nikki Giovanni, Daniel Lombardo, Michael Podesta, Jim Roberts, and Anne Soukhanov for their kind, generous, and very helpful suggestions about this book, I send bellflowers, emblems of gratitude and acknowledgement.

Opposite: SUSAN LOY. *The Language of Flowers*, 1986. Watercolor on paper, 15 1/2 x 15 1/2 inches.

The Language of Flowers

The red rose means love.

The Language of Flowers was formalized during Victorian times, when flowers came to represent particular sentiments; this tradition continues to this day, when for example, one might send red roses to a loved one.

WORTHINESS

JEALOUSY

CAMELLIA — EXCELLENCE

LILY OF THE VALLEY — RETURN OF HAPPINESS

TULIPS — DECLARATION OF LOVE

IRIS — INNOCENCE

WATER LILY — PURITY OF HEART

CARNATION — CAPRICIOUSNESS

ZINNIA — ABSENT FRIENDS

CHRYSANTHEMUM — CHEERFULNESS

DAHLIA — TREACHERY

MARIGOLD — DESPAIR

NARCISSUS — EGOTISM

NASTURTIUM — VICTORY

SUNFLOWER — HAUGHTINESS

ORIENTAL POPPY

GERANIUM — COMFORT

IRIS — SILENCE

ORCHID — MAGNIFICENCE

MORNING GLORY — ELOQUENCE

VIOLETS — MODESTY

PANSY — THOUGHTS

DEPARTURE

UNITY

GRACE

INTRODUCTION

This book grew out of my use of the historic language of flowers to create a series of Literary Calligraphy® watercolor paintings. The language of flowers is the tradition of associating flowers with sentiments or virtues – the red rose signifies love; rosemary stands for remembrance. I was first attracted to the language of flowers by virtues such as strength of character and loyalty, and I have been charmed by meanings like ambassador of love, hope in adversity, and return of happiness. The language of flowers provides a way to focus on a specific sentiment or virtue; the flower becomes an emblem for that quality or feeling.

The tradition of associating flowers and sentiments is ancient and universal. It was formalized during the Victorian era in England, France, and America with the publication of hundreds of language of flowers books during the nineteenth century. Language of flowers books contain a dictionary of flowers and their associated meanings, generally referred to as sentiments. They often include an additional dictionary of sentiments with their associated flowers. Most include sections of poetry either about flowers or about the sentiments they represent. Some books include botanical and horticultural information, plant lore, and other details about the plants. Some have floral calendars with flowers for each day of the year or sentiments for the week or month. A few include a fortune-telling system, referred to as a floral oracle. Many books contain illustrations, typically one to six color plates.

Flowers, the Angels' Alphabet follows the tradition of the language of flowers book. It features a dictionary of the American language of flowers and twenty-eight color reproductions of my Literary Calligraphy® watercolor paintings – part of my language of flowers series. The illustrations highlight chapters on twenty-four individual flowers. Each chapter includes a reproduction of one of my original watercolors – a hand-lettered presentation of the flower's sentiment from the language of flowers as well as a poem or verse that expresses that sentiment. In this way, for example, "the red rose means love," is accompanied by Robert Burns's poem, "My luve is like a red, red rose..." and surrounds a painting of the red rose. Four additional reproductions are large pieces that feature a total of 115 flowers. Three of these pieces contain alphabets of flowers, from Aster to Zinnia and Azalea to Zephyr Flower.

The dictionary of the American language of flowers has about 2,900 entries, which I have compiled from one dozen historic books published between 1832 and 1891 by American writers and publishers of the nineteenth century. It includes a vocabulary of some 1,400 flowers with their associated sentiments, and 1,500 sentiments and their associated flowers. I have edited the dictionary to eliminate some repetition, while retaining many of the subtle variations of meaning or flower type recorded by the nineteenth century writers.

When I first came to use the language of flowers for my art work, I was confronted with questions as to which flower a writer meant when he or she listed aster or bellflower, or what in the world is hackmetack? The appendix reflects my efforts to sort all of this out. Its 2,300 or so entries document the source of each flower's meaning as well as the botanical species identified by the writers of the nineteenth century. Because I use my dictionary to create alphabetic lists of flowers, the appendix includes extensive cross-references of flowers by common as well as botanical name. In addition to dictionaries from one dozen American books, it incorporates dictionaries from three British books by Shoberl, Tyas, and Greenaway, as well as a translation of Charlotte de Latour's listings from *Le Langage des Fleurs*.

I have compiled these dictionaries from books in my personal collection and from my research. I hand copied my first American dictionary in Alderman Library's rare book room at the University of Virginia. Subsequently I've searched for language of flowers books in antiquarian book shops throughout America, England, and Wales and, more recently, on the Internet.

The language of flowers has been called the angels' alphabet, a vocabulary of sentiments and virtues.

Flowers are the alphabet of angels, – whereby
They write on hills and fields mysterious truths.
John S. Adams, *Flora's Album*

This book is dedicated to the angels' alphabet.

THE HISTORY OF THE LANGUAGE OF FLOWERS BOOK

The language of flowers is primarily a literary tradition, based on *the language of flowers book* in Victorian England, France, and America. Such books are part of the genre of sentimental or gift flower books, which had its roots in the literary almanac, an annual publication that included a calendar. The language of flowers is based on a combination of folklore, literature, mythology, religion, and the physical characteristics of the plant.

Sources of flower associations that have made their way into Victorian language of flowers books include: ancient symbolic associations from Chinese, Japanese, Middle Eastern, Greek, and Roman cultures, mythologies, and religions; books such as herbals that recorded the virtues of plants as well as their myth and lore; literature, most notably Shakespeare; the Turkish language of flowers and objects, known as *selam*; and the plants themselves, often some distinguishing characteristic of the root, stem, leaf, bloom, or seed of the plant. Another source is the whim or fancy of the writer or editor.

One common misconception about the language of flowers is the belief that in the past there was one set of meanings which everyone knew. Although the inclination to associate flowers with sentiments or virtues is universal, there were many sets of meanings and significant cultural differences concerning the types of sentiments and flowers in the vocabulary. Nor was the language of flowers commonly practiced as a means of communication. There is little evidence that Victorian lovers used the language of flowers for secret communications. It has, however, been used by poets, writers, artists, and designers.

One of the most frequently mentioned sources of the language of flowers is the Turkish, Oriental, or Persian language of flowers or objects, referred to as *selam,* which was a system of memorization. Brent Elliott, Librarian to the Royal Horticultural Society, writes that the Turkish system was "not a language of *meanings*, but a mnemonic system – the names of the objects rhyme with standard lines of poetry, and are an aid by which the lines can be recalled." Indeed, Frederick Shoberl, the editor of *The Language of Flowers; with Illustrative Poetry* made the same claim in 1839:

Its spirit consists not, as might naturally be supposed, in the connection which fancy may trace between particular flowers and certain thoughts and feelings. Such an idea never entered the heads of the fair inventresses of the oriental language of flowers. They have contented themselves with merely taking a word which may happen to rhyme with the name of any particular flower or fruit, and then filling up the given rhyme with some fanciful phrase corresponding with its signification... Thus, for instance, the word Armonde (Pear) rhymes among other words with omonde (hope); and this rhyme is filled up as follows: –"Armonde – Wer banna bir omonde;" (Pear – Let me not despair.).

Thus it seems that *selam* was the source of a few flower associations, but not in the way originally intended. Modern writers cite *selam* as a source of flower sentiments and symbols, many of which correspond with the Victorian language of flowers.

Two individuals are credited with introducing the language of flowers to Europe – Seigneur Aubry de la Mottraye and Lady Mary Wortley Montagu. Mottraye's account of his visit to the court of Charles XII of Sweden, in exile in Turkey, was published in 1727, and immediately translated into English. Lady Mary Wortley Montagu accompanied her husband, the ambassador to Turkey, to his post in 1717. Her Turkish Embassy Letters were published in 1763, shortly after her death, and made her famous. The letters described Turkish life, including the language of objects.

The earliest literary record of the phrase "the language of flowers" may be Christopher Smart's line in *Jubilate Agno*, written during the period 1759 to 1763:

> For the flowers have their angels...
> For there is a language of flowers.
> For there is a sound reasoning upon all flowers.
> For elegant phrases are nothing but flowers.

By the early 1800's, "the language of flowers" was a commonly understood phrase in Europe. Handwritten lists were circulated in France. Beverly Seaton's *The Language of Flowers: A History* provides a useful account of the language of flowers book in England, France, and America. She indicates that the first language of flowers book was probably B. Delachenaye's *Abecedaire de Flore ou langage des fleurs,* published in 1810. The roots of the language of flowers book are in an old genre of books called almanacs. The literary almanac first included a calendar and was published as a New Year's gift book. Soon the calendar was dropped, making the book suitable for other occasions, and it evolved into the gift flower book. Literary annuals were published as early as 1765, in France, and 1770, in Germany, and reached their peak of popularity in Europe and America from about 1820 through mid-century.

The publication of Charlotte de Latour's *Le Langage des Fleurs* in December 1819 was the beginning of the great proliferation of language of flowers books. According to Seaton, Latour borrowed heavily from Alexis Lucot's *Emblemes de Flore*, published in January 1819. While Lacott's book was virtually unknown, Latour's was widely popular. Scholars agree that Charlotte de Latour was a pseudonym, but they are not sure of whom. The most frequently mentioned name is Louise Cortambert, wife of a well-known geographer, Eugene Cortambert.

Le Langage des Fleurs was published in several formats. According to Seaton,

> ...the smaller volume with fourteen plates and an engraved frontispiece sold for six francs, while the same volume with colored plates cost twelve francs. In larger format with colored plates the book cost twenty francs. The illustrations were by the famous miniaturist Pancrace Bessa. The publisher also produced...two special volumes: a small one printed on rose paper with the pictures on satin and a large one printed on vellum.

Latour's book stimulated the publishing industry, especially in France, England, and America, but also in Belgium, Germany and other European countries as well as in South America. Publishers from these countries produced hundreds of editions of language of flowers books during the nineteenth century.

The language of flowers reached England in the 1820's. Saunders and Otley published Henry Phillips' *Floral Emblems* in 1825, and Frederic Shoberl's *The Language of Flowers; With Illustrative Poetry* in 1834. A fifth American edition of Shoberl's book was published by Lea & Blanchard in 1839; its dictionary listings are included in the appendix. Shoberl was the editor of the popular annual "Forget Me Not" from 1822 to 1834.

Robert Tyas was another popular British flower writer, publisher, and clergyman who lived from 1811 to 1879. His book, *The Sentiment of Flowers; or, Language of Flora,* first published in 1836 and printed through the 1840's, was billed as an English version of Latour. The dictionary listings from the 1869 edition are included in the appendix.

One of the most familiar of language of flower books is the Routledge edition illustrated by Kate Greenaway, *The Language of Flowers*. First published in 1884, it continues to be reprinted to this day. The dictionary listings are included in the appendix. Greenaway, a respected and well-known writer and illustrator of children's books, lived in England from 1846 to 1901.

In the United States the first appearance of the language of flowers in print, according to Seaton, was in the writings of Constantine Samuel Rafinesque, a French-American naturalist, who wrote ongoing features under the title "The School of Flora," from 1827 through 1828, in the weekly *Saturday Evening Post* and the monthly *Casket; or Flowers of Literature, Wit, and Sentiment.* These pieces contained the botanic, English, and French names of the plant, a description of the plant, an explanation of its Latin names, and the flower's emblematic meaning.

During its peak in America, the language of flowers attracted the attention of the most popular women writers and editors of the day. A number of these American women who edited language of flowers books in the nineteenth century are represented in the American floral dictionary.

Sarah Josepha Hale edited *Flora's Interpreter* in 1832; it continued in print through the 1860's. She was editor of the *Ladies' Magazine* in Boston from 1828 to 1836 and co-editor of *Godey's Lady's Book,* from 1837 to 1877. *Godey's Lady's Book* was the most widely read periodical in the United States at the time. Hale is best known for her poem, "Mary Had a Little Lamb," published in 1830 in her book *Poems for Our Children.*

Catharine H. Waterman Esling wrote a long poem titled, "The Language of Flowers," which first appeared in 1839 in her own language of flowers book, *Flora's Lexicon*. It continued in print through the 1860's.

Lucy Hooper, an editor, novelist, poet, and playwright, included several of her flower poems in *The Lady's Book of Flowers and Poetry,* first published in 1841. She was associate editor at *Lippincott's Magazine*, a literary monthly, and a correspondent for the *Philadelphia Evening Telegraph.*

Frances Sargent Osgood, a poet and friend of Edgar Allen Poe, first published *The Poetry of Flowers and Flowers of Poetry* in 1841, and it continued in print through the 1860's. Osgood also edited a special gift book, *The Floral Offering,* in 1847. She was an editor of Snowden's *Ladies' Companion* from 1833 to 1844. Poe included her in his work of 1850, *The Literati.*

Sarah Carter Edgarton Mayo, author of several flower books, was associate editor of the Universalist monthly, *Ladies' Repository,* in Boston from 1839 to 1842. Her language of flowers book, *The Flower Vase,* was first published in 1844. She also edited the books *Fables of Flora* in 1844 and *The Floral Fortune Teller* in 1846.

C. M. Kirtland is probably Caroline Matilda Kirkland, editor of the *Union Magazine of Literature and Art* from 1847 to 1851 and the Unitarian weekly, *Christian Inquirer*, from 1847 to 1852. First published in 1848, her *Poetry of Flowers* continued to be in print at least until 1886. One of the more comprehensive works, the book's 522 pages contain an extensive dictionary and numerous flower poems.

Primarily because writers and editors copied each other's lists, there is a certain amount of agreement between French, English, and American floral vocabularies. Many of the language of flowers dictionaries were, therefore, direct or indirect descendants of Latour's *Le Langage des Fleurs.*

BIOGRAPHICAL NOTES

Several botanists, herbalists, and horticulturalists are referred to throughout this book.

THEOPHRASTUS (c. 372-287 B.C.). Considered the father of botany, this Greek philosopher was a student of Aristotle. His *Enquiry into Plants* was one of the first works of its kind in history.

PLINY (23-79). Gaius Plinius Secundus, or Pliny the Elder, wrote many books on Roman history, rhetoric, and natural science, but only his 37-volume *Natural History* has survived. It is a compilation of the writing of hundreds of Greek and Latin writers. Sixteen of the volumes concern the use of trees, plants, and flowers in medicine, farming, and cooking.

GERARD (1545-1612). John Gerard was an English herbalist. Published in 1597, his *Herball, or Generall Historie of Plantes* catalogued more than 1,000 species and was immensely popular. It was likely based on an English translation of the 1578 work of Flemish botanist Rembert Dodoens, *A Niewe Herball, or, Historie of Plantes,* which itself was based on previous herbals.

PARKINSON (1567-1650). John Parkinson became the royal apothecary and botanist to James I and Charles I. His 1629 book *Paradisi in Sole: Paradisus Terrestris* was one of the first great English books on garden flowers. *Paradisi in Sole* is a pun on Park-in-sun.

CULPEPER (1616-54). IN 1649 Nicholas Culpeper translated the *London Physical Directory*, which reflects the astrological school of medical botany. Five editions of his *English Physician Enlarged* were published before 1698, and the book continued to be published into the 1820's.

LINNAEUS (1707-78). Carolus Linnaeus was a Swedish botanist and founder of the binomial system of plant classification, which is still in use today.

BAILEY (1858-1954). Liberty Hyde Bailey is considered the dean of American horticulture. His *Standard Cyclopedia of Horticulture* catalogued the status of North American horticulture as it existed at the close of the nineteenth century.

AUTUMN CROCUS

Sentiment: Growing Old

Grow old along with me!
The best is yet to be,
The last of life, for which the first was made:
Our times are in His hand
Who saith "A whole I planned,
Youth shows but half; trust God: see all, nor be afraid!"

Robert Browning

Browning's long poem "Rabbi Ben Ezra" begins with these lines; it was published in 1864, three years after the death of his wife, Elizabeth Barrett Browning. Rabbi Ben Ezra was a Jewish scholar, born in Spain at the turn of the eleventh century, who mastered astronomy and physics and was a grammarian, philosopher, and poet. Browning has the rabbi speaking these now well-known lines about growing old.

Botanical Species: *Colchicum autumnale*
Common Names: autumn crocus, meadow saffron

Often confused with crocus, autumn crocus is actually a member of the lily family. Its botanical name, *Colchicum,* comes from Colchis, a country in Asia Minor, where it flourished. It is valued for its medicinal properties, particularly in the treatment of gout. The active principle is said to be an alkaline substance of a very poisonous nature called colchinine. An emblem of growing old, it blooms in the autumn of the year.

Description & Habitat: Long, dark green, lance-shaped leaves appear in early spring and usually die down by June. Crocus-like flowers arise in autumn from the root or *corm* and are light purple or white. It is like the spring-flowering, three-stamen crocus, except for its six stamens and autumn flowering habit. Gerard's *Herbal* described the meadow saffron: "It brings forth leaves in February, seed in May, and flowers in September, which is a thing clean contrary to all other plants whatsoever, for that they do first flower, and after seed; but this Saffron seeds first, and four months after brings forth flowers." A native of Europe and South Africa, it grows wild in meadows and is cultivated in America and elsewhere.

"Grow old along with me! The best is yet to be, The last of life, for which the first was made; Our times are in His hand Who saith, "A whole I planned, youth shows but half; trust God: see all, nor be afraid!" Robert Browning. In the language of flowers, the autumn crocus means growing old.

Susan Loy

CARNATION

Sentiment: Pride and Beauty

And let the beauty of the Lord our God be upon us: and establish thou the
work of our hands upon us; yea, the work of our hands establish thou it.

Psalms 90:17

This text speaks to beauty, to using the work of our hands to establish it, to taking pride in our work. Psalms were a popular form of poetry or song in the ancient Near East. The psalms of the Bible were probably written over a period of five centuries and edited in the fourth century B.C.

Botanical Species: *Dianthus caryophyllus*
Common Names: carnation, clove pink, gillyflower, grenadine, picotee, and pink

Theophrastus named this flower *Dianthus* about 300 B.C. from the Greek *dios,* of god or divine; and *anthos,* flower. *Caryophyllus* is from the Greek *caryon,* nut, and *phyllum,* leaf; this name had previously been given to the clove tree, so the carnation was given this name because of its clove-like scent. Some scholars think carnation is from *carnis,* for flesh, referring to the flesh-like color, while others think it is from *coronation* or *corone* because it was used in garlands.

Cultivated for more than 2,000 years, the carnation has more than 2,000 species and has rivaled the rose in commercial importance. Its development took off in the early 1600's and reached a peak in the early 1800's, when carnations were added to the select list of florists' flowers. According to American horticulturalist L. H. Bailey, "the American carnation," the perpetual-flowering carnation, actually originated in France about 1840, and was introduced to America in 1856, where it was improved by American growers. As a result of the flower's popularity, the American Carnation Society was formed in 1891.

Description & Habitat: These fragrant, mostly solitary, flowers have five broad petals with toothed edges that grow on stems with swollen joints and slender, opposite leaves. The flowers are often flesh-colored or pink but may be rose, purple, or white. Natives of the Mediterranean region, they are commonly grown as garden "pinks" in Europe and greenhouse "carnations" in America.

In the language of flowers, carnation means pride and beauty. "And let the beauty of the Lord our God be upon us: and establish thou the work of our hands upon us; yea, the work of our hands establish thou it." Psalms 90:17

Susan Loy

CHERRY

Sentiment: Education

Literae thesaurum est. Education is a treasure.
Gaius Petronius

When Roman novelist Gaius Petronius wrote these seemingly simple words in the first century, to be educated meant being literate, and a thesaurus was a treasure or treasury of words and knowledge. Writer Pamela Todd explains that the lore by which education became associated with the cherry alleges that Jesus gave a cherry to Saint Peter, instructing him to pay attention to detail and examine little things like the cherry.

Botanical species: *Prunus avium* and *Prunus cerasus*
Common Names: (*P. avium)* sweet or Mazzard cherry; (*P. cerasus)* Morello, pie, or sour cherry

Prunus is the ancient Latin name for plum and incorporates the stone fruits – plum, cherry, peach, nectarine, apricot, and almond. The Latin species name of the sweet cherry, *avium,* means "of birds." Its fruit is indeed a favorite of birds, and it is sometimes known as bird cherry. *Prunus cerasus* was introduced into Europe from ancient Cerasus, on the Crimean peninsula.

Sweet cherry trees rapidly spread throughout temperate Europe and Britain via birds and humans. Sour or pie cherry trees spread more slowly, mainly by human activity. Roman Lucius Lucullus brought sour cherry plants to Rome in 74 B.C. They were a gift from the city of Cerasus because it was known that Lucullus had acquired a fondness for them. By 1 A.D. Roman historian Pliny described ten types of cherries. Cultivated in Massachusetts only nine years after the Pilgrims arrived, cherry trees spread westward across North America with the settlers.

Description & Habitat: The sour cherry is a low round-headed tree with white flowers in small clusters mostly in advance of the oval leaves and red to purplish (sometimes yellow) fruit that matures in summer. There are several ornamental varieties, including a double-flowered form. It is a native of Asia Minor and perhaps southeast Europe. The sweet cherry is a tall robust tree with white flowers in dense clusters on spurs that appear with the young leaves; the shiny red fruit ripens in late spring and summer. It is a native of Europe and Western Asia.

LITTERA: A LETTER, ACQUAINTED WITH LETTERS, LITERATE, EDUCATED • THESAURUS: A TREASURE, TREASURY OF KNOWLEDGE, AS A DICTIONARY •

Education is a treasure. Litterae thesaurum est. Petronius • In the language of flowers, cherry means education.

S. Loy

DAFFODIL

Sentiment: Regard

Do unto others as you would have others do unto you.
The Golden Rule

The golden rule is universal. In Christianity it is recorded in Matthew 7:12; in Confucianism in Analects 15:23. It can also be found in Judaism, Buddhism, and Hinduism, and directs us to have regard for each other.

Botanical Species: *Narcissus pseudo-narcissus (N. major)*
Common Names: common daffodil, daffodil, trumpet daffodil, lent lily

The name daffodil probably comes from "affodyle," an old English word meaning early-comer, a corruption of the Greek word for asphodel. A daffodil and a narcissus differ as to the length of the trumpet and the number of flowers per stem. All daffodils are narcissi, but not all narcissi are daffodils.

The botanical name, *Narcissus,* according to some scholars, comes not from the youth of classical mythology, but from the Greek word *narkao,* to benumb, because of the plant's narcotic properties. Pliny wrote, "Narce narcissum dictum, non a fabuloso puero" – Narcissus is named from Narce, not from the fabulous boy. Yet the myth persists that Narcissus died, literally in vain, trying to embrace his own reflection in the water, and that on the spot where his dead body had lain bloomed a new flower which was given the name narcissus.

Narcissi are among the oldest of cultivated plants. They were grown by Egyptians some 3,000 years ago and remain to this day one of the most popular spring flowers.

Description & Habitat: Long and narrow leaves usually appear in early spring with the yellow or white flowers, which grow from bulbs on tall stems. The long, trumpet-shaped corona lends its name to the trumpet daffodil. The plant is twelve to eighteen inches tall, and the leaves reach the two-inch-long flower. Daffodils are exceedingly variable in size, shape, and color and include double and bi-color forms. According to horticulturalist L. H. Bailey, *N. pseudo-narcissus* came from England and Sweden to Spain and Austria. It grows wild in most European countries.

Do unto others as you would have others do unto you. The Golden Rule. In the language of flowers, daffodil means regard.

S. Loy

DAISY

Sentiment: Innocence

I'd choose to be a daisy,
If I might be a flower,
Closing my petals softly
At twilight's quiet hour;
And waking in the morning,
When falls the early dew,
To welcome Heaven's bright sunshine,
And Heaven's bright teardrops, too.

This anonymous poem can be found in many of the old anthologies. The daisy has long been the children's flower, an emblem of innocence.

Botanical Species: *Bellis perennis*
Common Names: daisy, English daisy, marguerite

Its botanical name is from the Latin, *bellus,* pretty. Daisy is from the Saxon word meaning day's eye, or eye of the day. It is quite true to its name, for it opens its petals in the morning and folds them when the sun goes down. Daisy is a name applied to many flowers of the Composite family. There are about ten species of *Bellis*, only one of which is American, *Bellis integrifolia.* The plant that is most commonly called daisy in America is *Chrysanthemum leucanthemum,* also named ox-eye daisy.

In Britain and America, girls have recited the popular refrain, "He loves me; he love me not," while pulling petals from this flower until the last petal provides the answer.

Description & Habitat: The daisy, as it grows wild in England, has a yellow center, surrounded by numerous rays in a single row, but many cultivated forms are double, the rays rising in tiers, crowding out the yellow center. The English daisy is essentially a pinkish flower in appearance; the under-surfaces and sometimes the tips of the white rays are pink or red. A low perennial, the daisy grows wild in western Europe and has been naturalized in England. Because it thrives in cool, moist atmospheres, it has been more popular in England than America.

In the language of flowers, the daisy means innocence. "I'd choose to be a daisy; if I might be a flower, closing my petals softly at twilight's quiet hour; In the early dew, to welcome Heaven's bright sunshine, and Heaven's bright teardrops too." Anonymous. and waking in the morning, when falls the early dew, to welcome Heaven's

FENNEL

Sentiment: Worthy of Praise

For the beauty of the earth, for the glory of the skies,
For the love which from our birth over and around us lies:
For the beauty of each hour of the day and of the night,
Hill and vale, and tree and flower, sun and moon and stars of light:

For the joy of ear and eye, for the heart and mind's delight,
For the mystic harmony linking sense to sound and sight:
For the joy of human love, brother, sister, parent, child,
Friends on earth and friends above; for all gentle thoughts and mild:

Lord of all to thee we raise this our hymn of grateful praise.

The words to the hymn "For the Beauty of the Earth" were written by Folliott Sanford Pierpont, an American who lived from 1835 to 1917.

Botanical Species: *Foeniculum vulgare*
Common Name: fennel, wild fennel

Linnaeus first named fennel *Anethum foeniculum,* embracing two varieties – sweet fennel and common or wild fennel. Later botanists placed it with *Foeniculum*, which means little hay – the name given to this plant by the Romans because of its hay-like odor – dividing it into two varieties, *F. vulgare,* common or wild fennel, and *F. dulce*, sweet fennel.

Fennel was cultivated by the ancient Romans for its edible leaves, seeds, and stalks, which taste like licorice. Pliny may have started the superstition that fennel strengthens the eyes. It was included in ancient victory wreaths as a symbol of strength and that which is worthy of praise.

Description & Habitat: A tall herb, with delicate, feathery leaves that grow from the edible root stalk. The small, yellow flowers, produced in terminal clusters on up to twenty rays, resemble the flowers of the dill plant. Considered indigenous to the Mediterranean region, it has spread with civilization and may be found growing wild in many parts of the world. It flourishes particularly in limestone soils near the sea.

For the beauty of the earth, for the beauty of each hour, of the day and of the night, Hill and vale, and tree and flower, sun and moon and stars of light: For the glory of the skies, For the love which from our birth over and around us lies: This our hymn of grateful praise. Pierpoint In the human love, parent, child, sister, brother, friends on earth and friends above; for all gentle thoughts and mild: For the joy of human love, For the joy of ear and eye, For the heart and mind's delight, For the mystic harmony Linking sense to sound and sight: For the joy of flower fennel means Lord of all to thee we raise

Susan Loy

GLADIOLUS

Sentiment: Ready Armed or Strength of Character

We never know how high we are
Till we are asked to rise
And then if we are true to plan
Our statures touch the skies –
The Heroism we recite
Would be a common thing
Did not ourselves the cubits warp
For fear to be a king

Emily Dickinson

Emily Dickinson wrote this poem about strength of character around 1870.

Botanical Species: *Gladiolus species*
Common Name: glad, gladiolus, corn-flag, sword-flag

Gladioli were known in ancient Greece and Rome. The name gladiolus comes from the Latin, *gladium,* a sword. For the ancient Romans, a gladiolus was a little sword used by gladiators. Pliny applied the word gladiolus to the flower because of its long, sword-shaped leaves. The ancient Greek name for the gladiolus was *xiphium*, from *xiphos*, a sword. Its sentiment in the language of flowers, ready armed or strength of character, relates to its ancient meaning.

Gladioli were imported from South Africa in large quantities by the end of the eighteenth century. Since that time, the genus *Gladiolus* has been greatly altered by hybridization; many new forms and colors have been developed. The American Gladiolus Society was founded in 1910, in Boston, to test new varieties, develop a standard nomenclature, and promote interest in the flower.

Description & Habitat: The gladiolus is an excellent cut flower. Flower stalks grow to about two feet from bulbs. In summer and autumn, the large, funnel-shaped tubular flowers grow around the stalk for nearly half its length with the lower ones blooming first. Colors range from white, pastel pink, orange and lavender, to bright yellow, red, and purple. There are more than 160 species, the majority being from South Africa.

IN THE LANGUAGE OF
FLOWERS, GLADIOLUS MEANS
STRENGTH OF CHARACTER.

WE NEVER KNOW HOW HIGH
WE ARE TILL WE ARE ASKED TO
RISE AND THEN IF WE ARE
TRUE TO PLAN OUR STATURES
TOUCH THE SKIES-THE HEROISM
WE RECITE WOULD BE A
COMMON THING DID NOT
OURSELVES THE CUBITS
WARP FOR FEAR TO BE A
KING— EMILY DICKINSON

IRIS

Sentiment: Message

Thou art the Iris, fair among the fairest,
Who, armed with golden rod
And winged with the celestial azure, bearest
The Message of some God.

Thou art the Muse, who far from crowded cities
Hauntest the sylvan streams,
Playing on pipes of reed the artless ditties
That come to us as dreams.

O flower-de-luce, bloom on, and let the river
Linger to kiss thy feet!
O flower of song, bloom on, and make for ever
The world more fair and sweet.

Henry Wadsworth Longfellow, "Flower-de-Luce"

Longfellow wrote "Flower-de-Luce" on March 20, 1860. As this poem shows, he was well-schooled in classical mythology and flower lore and knew that iris means message.

Botanical Name: *Iris species*
Common Names: flag, fleur-de-lis (fleur de luce, flower-de-Lys, flower-de-luce), iris

The plant was named for the goddess Iris, who traveled over her rainbow bridge carrying messages. Like the rainbow, the plant comes in a wide variety of colors, in more than one hundred species. Iris is one of the oldest cultivated plants; bearded irises have been known since antiquity. Longfellow's iris was probably *I. versicolor*, also called blue flag, or flower-de-luce. Found in eastern North America, it was introduced to England in 1732.

Description & Habitat: These showy perennials have mostly long slender basal leaves. White, yellow, or purple flowers with three sepals and petals grow at the tips of erect stalks. The many iris species include German or bearded irises such as *I. germanica, I. florentina;* Japanese irises; tall irises such as *I. siberica;* dwarf irises such as *I. versicolor;* and bulbous irises. Irises are native to temperate North America, Europe, Asia, and North Africa.

In the language of flowers, the iris means message. "Thou art the Iris, fair among the fairest, who, armed with golden rod and winged with the celestial azure, bearest the message of some God. Thou art the Muse, who, far away from crowded cities hauntest the sylvan streams, playing on pipes of reed the artless ditties that come to us as dreams, O flower-de-luce, bloom on, and let the river linger to kiss thy feet! O flower of song, bloom on, and make forever the world more fair and sweet." Henry Wadsworth Longfellow

Susan Loy

Iris versicolor

IVY

Sentiment: Friendship

I awoke this morning with devout thanksgiving for my friends, the old and the new.

Ralph Waldo Emerson, "Friendship"

Emerson's essay "Friendship" was part of *Essays, First Series*, originally published in 1841. Emerson worked out many of the themes of this essay in letters to his friends, including Margaret Fuller, co-editor with Emerson of *The Dial,* a literary magazine. Emerson's major theme in this essay was the celebration of friendship.

Botanical Species: *Hedera helix*
Common Names: common ivy, English ivy, ivy

Hedera is the ancient Latin name of ivy, which some say is derived from the Celtic *haedra,* a cord. The derivation of the English word *ivy* is unclear. Some trace it to *iw*, which is Old English for green. Although it was a garden plant grown by the ancients, not much has been written about its history.

The ancients used ivy leaves to make the poet's crown and sometimes the crown of Bacchus, although at other times his crown was made with grape leaves to represent him as the god of wine. In Greece, the marriage altar was surrounded with ivy, and the priest presented a sprig of ivy to newly-married couples. Because of its clinging habit, ivy has long been regarded as an emblem of fidelity and lasting friendship.

Description & Habitat: This evergreen vine climbs by means of fibers resembling roots that shoot out all along the woody stem; the fibers have small disks at the end, which adapt themselves to the surface on which the plant climbs. When the vine gets to the top of a tree or wall, the shiny green leaves change from five-lobed and angular to oval without lobes. Ivy produces its inconspicuous greenish flowers when the branches get above their support. It is native to the greater part of Europe, North Africa and Asia and is hardy in North America as far north as Massachusetts.

"I awoke this morning with devout thanksgiving for my friends, the old and the new." Ralph Waldo Emerson, "Friendship." • In the language of flowers, ivy means friendship. • "

LADY'S SLIPPER

Sentiment: Capricious Beauty

Glory be to God for dappled things –
For skies of couple-colour as a brinded cow;
For rose-moles all in stipple upon trout that swim;
Fresh-firecoal chestnut falls; finches' wings;
Landscape plotted and pieced – fold, fallow, and plough;
And all trades, their gear and tackle and trim.
All things counter, original, spare, strange;
Whatever is fickle, freckled (who knows how?)
With swift, slow; sweet, sour; adazzle, dim;
He fathers-forth whose beauty is past change:
Praise him.

> Gerard Manley Hopkins, "Pied Beauty"

What better flower to express the sentiment of capricious beauty than the freckled yellow lady's slipper, and what better poem than "Pied Beauty," written in 1877, by British poet Gerard Manley Hopkins. Capricious means subject to whim; unpredictable; fickle. Pied means having patches or blotches; piebald; freckled. The yellow lady's slipper is the only lady's slipper native to Britain.

Botanical Species: *Cypripedium calceolus, C. pubscens*
Common Names: American valerian, lady's slipper, moccasin flower, Venus' slipper, yellow lady's slipper

Cypripedium means Venus' slipper. Venus was commonly called Cyprus because she was born off the shores of Cyprus; *pedilon* means sandal or slipper; thus, Venus' slipper. Flemish botanist Dodoens named the yellow lady's slipper *Calceolus marianus* in 1554. Linnaeus changed the name to *Cypripedium* in the eighteenth century. Clergyman and botanist John Banister wrote from Virginia in 1669 of three kinds of lady's slippers, called moccasin flowers because they resembled the Indians' shoes of that name.

Description & Habitat: A pair of leaves, long and leafy or close to the ground, surround a short stem with a usually solitary terminal flower with brownish-purple sepals and petals and a large yellow freckled pouch. The petals are usually twisted and narrower than the sepals. The yellow lady's slipper is native to North America, Europe, and Asia.

In the language of flowers, the lady slipper means capricious beauty.

"Glory be to God for dappled things—for skies of couple-colour as a brinded cow; for rose-moles all in stipple upon trout that swim; fresh-firecoal chestnut-falls; finches' wings; landscape plotted and pieced—fold, fallow, and plough; And all trades, their gear and tackle and trim. All things counter, original, spare, strange; whatever is fickle, freckled (who knows how?) with swift, slow; sweet, sour; adazzle, dim; he fathers-forth, whose beauty is past change. Praise him." "Pied Beauty,"

Gerard Manley Hopkins

Susan Loy

LEMON GERANIUM

Sentiment: Serenity

*God, grant me the serenity to accept the things I cannot change,
the courage to change the things I can, and the wisdom to know the difference.*

The Serenity Prayer is attributed to Reinhold Niebuhr, an American theologian, who taught at the Union Theological Seminary from 1928 to 1960. The prayer is widely attributed to Niebuhr, if not credited outright, but one editor suggests that the prayer is from eighteenth-century Germany. One of Niebuhr's biographers indicates that Niebuhr delivered his sermons extemporaneously, and the prayer was first published in 1951.

Botanical Species: *Pelargonium limoneum*
Common Names: lemon geranium, lemon-scented geranium, pelargonium

Pelargonium is named from *pelargos*, stork, because its long, slender seed pod resembles a stork's bill. Named by the Greek physician Dioscorides, geranium comes from *geranos*, meaning crane, referring to the seed pod, which resembles a crane's beak.

Pelargonium is distinguished from geranium by technical characteristics. The flowers of geranium are mostly regular, while those of pelargonium are irregular, and the two upper petals differ in size, shape and color. Pelargoniums have a nectar-bearing tube, which geraniums do not. Lemon geranium is one of various scented-leaved pelargoniums, often known collectively as "rose geraniums." *P. limoneum* is a garden hybrid sometimes known as *P. odoratum*; *P. crispum* is probably one of its parents. There is also a form with variegated leaves; the old-fashioned variety known as Lady Mary is of this group.

Description & Habitat: This much-branched, woody plant has lemon-scented leaves, mostly three-lobed with toothed edges. The pink to purple flowers are irregular with five petals, the two upper usually larger, the lower narrow. The flower is formed at the base of a slender nectar-bearing tube. Found originally in South Africa, they are popular bedding flowers as well as pot plants for both indoors and out.

In the language of flowers, lemon geranium means serenity. "God, grant me the serenity to accept the things I cannot change, the courage to change the things I can, and the wisdom to know the difference." Attributed to Reinhold Niebuhr

LILY OF THE VALLEY

Sentiment: Return of Happiness

This is the day that the Lord hath made; we will rejoice and be glad in it.

Psalms 118:24

Psalms are a popular book from the Old Testament; they are songs and are among the most poetic verses in the Bible. This verse expresses each day's promise of a return of happiness.

Botanical Species: *Convallaria majalis*
Common Name: conval lily, lily of the valley, May lily, *muget*

Lily of the valley's old name was *Lilium convallarium*, derived from *convallis*, a valley; thus, lily of the valley. The species name *majalis* or *maialis* signifies that which belongs to May. John Gerard, an English herbalist, wrote, "it is called in English Lillie of the Valley, or the Conval Lillie, and the May Lillies."

English physician Nicholas Culpepper wrote in 1826 that lilies of the valley "grow plentifully upon Hampstead heath," but herbalist Maud Grieve later reported that since the trees on Hampstead Heath, near London, were destroyed in the 1830's, "it has been but sparingly found there." According to American horticulturalist L. H. Bailey, by 1900 lilies of the valley were cultivated in large quantities in Germany for the export trade; millions reached the United States.

British legend says that the fragrance of the lily of the valley attracts the nightingale out of the hedgerow and leads him to his mate in the recesses of the valley.

Description & Habitat: This perennial is much prized for its erect racemes of white, scented flowers, which bloom in May. In early spring, quill-like pips emerge from underground stems; as the pips lengthen and uncoil they appear as two leaves. At the back of the leaves is the short flower stalk, bearing several buds near its top which are greenish when young, becoming pure white bells as they open and turn downward, with the petals turned back, forming six small scallops. Native to Europe, Asia, and parts of North America, lilies of the valley run wild along shady roadsides and in neglected gardens; these hardy plants are easily grown in partially shaded places.

This is the day which the Lord hath made; we will rejoice and be glad in it. Psalms 118:24 In the language of flowers, lily of the valley means return of happiness.

MAGNOLIA

Sentiment: Love of Nature

If I were to name the three most precious resources of life, I should say books, friends, and nature; and the greatest of these, at least the most constant and always at hand is nature. Nature we have always with us, an inexhaustible storehouse of that which moves the heart, appeals to the mind, and fires the imagination, – health to the body, a stimulus to the intellect, and joy to the soul.

John Burroughs, "Leaf and Tendril"

John Burroughs lived from 1837 to 1921 and was a contemporary of fellow nature writer John Muir. For ten years he worked in Washington, D.C., where he became friends with Walt Whitman. His first book, *Notes on Walt Whitman, Poet and Person*, was published in 1867. He returned in 1873 to New York's Catskill Mountains, near where he was born, and lived on a small farm overlooking the Hudson River. There he wrote dozens of books and essays about nature.

Botanical Species: *Magnolia grandiflora*
Botanical Names: bull bay, evergreen magnolia, magnolia, southern magnolia

Magnolia was named after Pierre Magnol (1638-1715), a professor of medicine and director of the botanic garden at Montpellier, France. Magnolias are an ancient tree, but the earliest magnolias to reach Europe came from America. Clergyman and botanist John Banister sent a Virginia magnolia to Europe in 1688.

Because the large blossoms bruise so easily, messages can be inscribed with a pointed instrument on the large petals; the letters soon become apparent. Magnolia is one of the most beautiful native American trees and a worthy representative of love of nature.

Description & Habitat: This evergreen tree has a straight trunk. Its thick, oblong leaves are shiny bright green above and pale beneath with rust-colored hairs. The very fragrant, very large white flowers are cup-shaped, about eight inches in diameter with three white sepals and six to twelve petals that appear in late spring and summer. The cone-shaped fruit are pink to brown in color and are about three inches long. Magnolias are native to Asia and America but not Europe. *Magnolia grandiflora* is native to the Gulf Coast and southern Atlantic Coast states.

In the language of flowers, magnolia means love of nature. "If I were to name the three most precious resources of life, I should say books, friends, and nature; and the greatest of these, at least the most constant and always at hand, is nature. Nature we have always with us, an inexhaustible storehouse of that which moves the heart, appeals to the mind, and fires the imagination, — health to the body, a stimulus to the intellect, and joy to the soul." John Burroughs, Leaf and Tendril.

Susan Loy

MINT

Sentiment: Virtue

The flowers of the earth do not grudge at one another,
though one be more beautiful and fuller of virtue than another;
but they stand kindly by one another, and enjoy one another's virtue.

Jakob Boehme

Jakob Boehme was a German mystic who lived from 1575 to 1624. Following a mystical experience in 1600, he waited twelve years before committing his vision to writing. He wrote other works and was eventually banished on a charge of impiety from his native town to Dresden, where he would one day be received by the emperor at a meeting of "eminent divines."

Botanical Species: *Mentha viridis (M. spicata)*
Common Names: garden mint, mint, spearmint, spire mint

Theophrastus named mint for Menthe, a nymph who, because of the love Pluto bore her, was changed by a jealous Proserpine into the plant we now call mint. *Viridis* is Latin for green; *spicata* means spiked: hence spearmint. Mint has been so universally esteemed that it can be found nearly everywhere civilization has extended and is an apt emblem for virtue.

The garden mint was cultivated by ancient Romans and other Mediterraneans. There are references to it in Pliny's writings and in the Bible. The Romans introduced it to Britain. The Pilgrims introduced it to America. John Josselyn was one of the first colonial visitors to describe the plants of New England; mint appears on one of his lists of plants brought to America.

Description and Habitat: This strong-scented perennial herb has a square stem that rises to about two feet, bearing smooth, bright green leaves with finely toothed edges. The small pinkish or lilac-colored, bell-shaped, lipped flowers are densely arranged in rings off the stems of the upper leaves and form cylindrical, tapering spikes. Native to Europe and Asia, mint can be found throughout the world, often growing wild.

In the language of flowers, mint means virtue. "The flowers of the earth do not grudge at one another, though one be more beautiful and fuller of virtue than another; but they stand kindly one by another, and enjoy one another's virtue." Jakob Boehme, c. 1600

OLIVE

Sentiment: Peace

Lord, make me an instrument of Thy peace.
Where there is hatred, let me sow love;
Where there is injury, pardon;
Where there is doubt, faith;
Where there is despair, hope;
Where there is darkness, light;
And where there is a sadness, joy.

The Prayer of St. Francis of Assisi

In 1208 in Italy, St. Francis of Assisi founded the Franciscan order, a group devoted to living a life of peace.

Botanical Species: *Olea europea*
Common Name: olive, olive tree

Olea is the classical name for olive. Olive was sacred to the Roman goddess Minerva and to the Greek goddess Athene. The story of the dove returning to Noah's Ark with an olive branch as a signal of peace in the land is one of the most famous of the Old Testament. The olive, to quote the poet Sarah Josepha Hale, "has been, since the Deluge, the emblem of peace."

The ancients used olive oil for food and medicine, as well as for anointing their bodies and as fuel in oil lamps. Phoenicians, Greeks, and Romans introduced the cultivation of olives into all Mediterranean countries, and the Spanish introduced olives to Mexico and California.

Description & Habitat: The olive tree is small, rarely exceeding 25 feet, bearing small oblong leaves and forking panicles of creamy white fragrant flowers. The tiny flowers have a short tube and petals with four lobes. The fruit is a small oval "drupe." (A drupe is a fleshy one-seeded fruit with the seed enclosed in a stone.) The fleshy part of the olive is filled with oil; up to sixty percent of a ripe olive is oil. The olive tree is probably native to the eastern Mediterranean region and Asia Minor and has been cultivated for its oil for more than 5,000 years. An olive is green when immature; it turns purple, then black as it ripens. The fruit is picked early for green olives. For black olives it is allowed to mature on the tree but not to become too soft. The fruit is allowed to fully ripen for olive oil.

In • Lord, make me an instrument of Thy peace. Where there is hatred, let me sow love; where there is injury, pardon; where there is doubt, faith; where there is despair, hope; where there is darkness, light; and where there is sadness, joy.... Prayer of St. Francis of Assisi • olive means Peace. • In the language of flowers,

Susan Loy

PANSY

Sentiment: Thoughts

Whatever is true, whatever is honorable, whatever is just, whatever is pure, whatever is lovely, whatever is gracious, if there is any excellence, if there is anything worthy of praise, think about these things.

Philippians 4:8

These words of advice from St. Paul's letter to the Philippians, an early treatise on the power of positive thinking, are among my favorites.

Botanical Name: *Viola tricolor*
Common Names: heartsease, *herb trinitatis*, Johnny-jump-up, love-in-idleness, pansy, *pensée*, wild pansy

The word *pansy* is a corruption of the French word *pensée* meaning thoughts, so named because of the plant's habit of hanging its head as if in a pensive or thoughtful mood. Pansy's showy flower is often likened to a face. This flower has had many names. In some of the old herbals the pansy was called *herb trinitatis*, being dedicated to the trinity because of its three colors. Elizabethans called them heartsease or love in idleness as well as pansies. In ancient days the plant was much used in love charms, and English herbalist Maud Grieve suggests that may be the origin of the name heartsease. Johnny-jump-up is a shortening of the English name, jump-up-and-kiss-me.

Viola tricolor is the ancestor of our modern pansy. It is an old garden flower, described by the English herbalist John Gerard in 1587, and by botanist John Parkinson in 1629. According to horticulturalist L. H. Bailey, a certain T. Thompson, gardener to a British lord, bred the ancestor of our modern garden pansies in 1810, developing the first "blotched" pansy.

Description & Habitat: All violas are highly variable, but pansies can be distinguished from other violas by their free-branching stems and by their leaves, which have rounded lobes. *Viola tricolor* has five parts as to sepals, petals, and stamens; the lower petal of the flower is spurred; the other four are in two symmetrical pairs. The three colors of its name are purple, yellow, and white; the upper petals are generally purple, while the lowest and broadest are yellow and white. The modern garden pansy is much larger than its ancestor and comes in many colors. *V. tricolor* probably originated in Europe. Pansies thrive in cool moist climates like those in England, Scotland and northern Europe.

"whatever is true, whatever is honorable, whatever is just, whatever is pure, whatever is lovely, whatever is gracious, if there is any excellence, if there is anything worthy of praise, think about these things." Philippians 4:8. In the language of flowers, pansies mean any thoughts.

RED ROSE

Sentiment: Love

O, my luve is like a red, red rose, That's newly sprung in June,
O, my love is like a melodie, That's sweetly play'd in tune.
As fair art thou, my bonie lass, So deep in luve am I,
And I will luve thee still my dear, Till a' the seas gang dry.

Till a' the seas gang dry, my dear, And the rocks melt wi' the sun!
And I will luve thee still, my dear, While the sands a life shall run.
And fare thee weel, my only luve! And fare thee weel, a while!
And I will come again, my luve, Tho it were ten thousand mile!

Robert Burns

This poem by Robert Burns was published in 1794, shortly before his death at the age of 37. The text is actually an amalgam of several old ballads and illustrates Burns's genius for reworking Scottish folk material.

Botanical Species: *Rosa gallica*
Common Names: apothecary rose, red Provins rose, red rose, rose

The rose's name refers to its color: *rosa* is Latin for red. *Gallica* means of Gaul or France. Despite this latter appellation, the birthplace of the cultivated rose was probably Persia, not France; it spread across the Middle East to Greece and from Greece to Italy. Pliny and others describe in detail the cultivation of roses in ancient times. Associated with Aphrodite and Venus, goddesses of love and beauty, roses were worn by ancient Roman brides and bridegrooms. Cupid covered Mars and Venus's bed with roses, and Christopher Marlowe's passionate shepherd also made a "bed of roses."

Description & Habitat: This upright shrub grows up to five feet high and has stems densely covered with prickles. The oval green leaves with finely toothed edges grow three to five per stem. The deep pink to red, fragrant flowers are two to three inches across, growing on stout upright prickly stems. Five petals and sepals, which bend back during flowering, are enclosed in an urn-shaped receptacle. The receptacle is berry-like at maturity, containing many fruits called "hips." The rose is a native of central and southern Europe and western Asia.

In the language of flowers, the red rose means love. "O, my luve is like a red, red rose, the red rose means love. "O, my luve is like a red, red rose, That's newly sprung in June, O my luve is like the melodie, That's sweetly play'd in tune. As fair art thou, my bonie lass, So deep in luve am I, And I will luve thee still, my dear, Till a' the seas gang dry. Till a' the seas gang dry, my dear, And the rocks melt wi' the sun! And I will luve thee still, my dear, While the sands o' life shall run. And fare thee weel, my only luve! And fare thee weel, a while! And I will come again, my luve, Tho' it were ten thousand mile." R. Burns

RED TULIP

Sentiment: Declaration of Love

Come live with me, and be my love, And we will all the pleasures prove
That valleys, groves, hills, and fields, Woods or steepy mountain yields.
And we will sit upon the rocks, Seeing the shepherds feed their flocks,
By shallow rivers, to whose falls, Melodious birds sing madrigals.

And I will make thee beds of roses, With a thousand fragrant posies,
A cap of flowers, and a kirtle, Embroidered all with leaves of myrtle.
A belt of straw and ivy buds, With coral clasps and amber studs:
And if these pleasures may thee move, Come live with me, and be my love.

Christopher Marlowe

Christopher Marlowe's "The Passionate Shepherd to His Love" has survived in several manuscript and printed versions. This modern language rendition is based on the four-stanza version, printed in *The Passionate Pilgrim*, 1599, and in *Helicon*, 1600.

Botanical species: *Tulipa gesneriana*
Common Names: red tulip, common garden tulip, Darwin tulip, late tulip

The Austrian ambassador to Turkey brought the first tulip seeds to Vienna in 1554, and they rapidly disseminated throughout Europe. The name *tulip* is considered to be the Latinized name of the Persian word for turban, *dulband*. It has been reported that the ambassador mistook the name of the flower for that of the turbans into which tulips were tucked, or that he thought tulips resembled inverted turbans. The common garden tulip is derived from *Tulipa gesneriana,* named by Linnaeus for Swiss botanist Konrad Gesner, who described tulips growing in Augsburg as early as 1559. The herbalist Clusius of Artois is credited with introducing tulips into England in 1577, and by the 1630's the flower's popularity gave rise to "tulipomania" in Holland.

Description & Habitat: Mostly single flowers arise directly from the bulb on an erect stem, six to twenty-four inches tall. The leaves are long and narrow or broad, often undulated. The erect, rarely nodding, bell-shaped flower has six bright red or varicolored oval petals that are rounded at the tip; when bright red, it has only an obscure basal blotch. Tulips are native to Turkey and the Mediterranean countries.

In the language of flowers, the red tulip means declaration of love. "Come live with me and be my love, and we will all the pleasures prove That valleys, groves, hills and fields, woods, or steepy mountain yields. And we will sit upon the rocks, seeing the shepherds feed their flocks, By shallow rivers, to whose falls melodious birds sing madrigals. And I will make thee beds of roses, and a thousand fragrant posies, A cap of flowers, and a kirtle, embroider'd all with leaves of myrtle; A belt of straw and ivy-buds, with coral clasps and amber studs, And if these pleasures may thee move, come live with me, and be my love."

Christopher Marlowe, "The Passionate Shepherd to His Love."

Susan Loy

ROSEMARY

Sentiment: Remembrance

There's rosemary, that's for remembrance; pray you, love, remember.
William Shakespeare

This line spoken by Ophelia in *Hamlet, Act IV, Scene V* is one of the most famous literary examples of the language of flowers.

Botanical Species: *Rosmarinus officinalis*
Common Name: rosemary

In Latin, *Rosmarinus* means sea dew. The name was probably given because of the plant's fondness for the sea air. *Officinalis* means that it is official, medicinal, recognized in the pharmacopoeia. In place of more costly incense, the ancients used rosemary in their religious ceremonies; an old French name for it was *Incensier*.

Rosemary became the emblem of remembrance because it had a reputation for strengthening the memory. At ancient weddings, it was entwined in the wreath worn by the bride, and it's alleged that Anne of Cleves wore such a wreath at her wedding. Rosemary branches, gilded and tied with colorful ribbons, were presented to wedding guests as a symbol of love and fidelity. Rosemary sprigs were once placed in the dock of courts of justice to improve the memory.

In his plays, Ben Johnson alluded to the custom of giving rosemary, together with a clove-studded orange, at New Year's. In *The Garden,* Robert Herrick recorded its use in Christmas decorations. Sir Thomas More wrote, "As for Rosmarine, I lett it runne all over my garden walls, not onlie because my bees love it, but because it is the herb sacred to remembrance, and, therefore, to friendship."

Description & Habitat: This evergreen shrub grows to four feet high with numerous, very narrow aromatic leaves about one inch long. The leaves are dark blue-green above and paler beneath. The tiny light bluish-purple flowers appear in short racemes at the axils. The tiny flowers are two-lipped and three-toothed, giving them a ruffled effect. Cultivated for its herb and oil, rosemary is indigenous to Europe, China, and Asia Minor.

There's rosemary, that's for remembrance; pray you, love, remember — Shakespeare, Hamlet. In the language of flowers, rosemary means remembrance.

SNOWBALL

Sentiment: Thoughts of Heaven

To see the World in a Grain of Sand,
And Heaven in a Wild Flower,
Hold infinity in the palm of your hand,
An eternity in an hour.
> William Blake, "Auguries of Innocence"

There are several published versions of Blake's poem, each with subtle variations. The word before World has been published as "a" and as "the," and the word before eternity has been published as "an" as well as "and." Blake wrote this poem during the period he lived at Felpham, on the Sussex coast, from 1800 to 1803. He was an engraver, painter, and poet who published several books of his own poetry and illuminations.

Botanical Species: *Viburnum opulus, V. roseum*
Common Names: guelder rose, high bush cranberry, red or rose elder, snowball, snowball tree

Viburnum, meaning the wayfaring tree, is snowball's ancient Latin name. Chaucer recommended eating the raw berries, but apparently they are quite bitter. In Siberia, the berries have been fermented with flour and a spirit distilled from them. In Norway and Sweden, they have been used to flavor a paste of honey and flour. In Canada, they have been substituted for cranberries in a piquant jelly, thereby gaining the name high bush cranberry. The name guelder rose comes from the Dutch province where the tree was first cultivated. Its globe-shaped flower clusters resemble snowballs.

Description & Habitat: This shrub grows up to twelve feet with smooth light grey branches and stems. The broad, three-lobed oval leaves are up to four inches long. In late spring and summer, tiny white bell-shaped flowers form large globe-shaped clusters on stems. A major difference between *V. opulus* and *V. roseum* is that *V. roseum* is a showy but sterile flower that lacks the decorative fruit or drupe of *V. opulus*, which quickly turns scarlet. *Viburnum opulus* and *Viburnum roseum* are native to Europe, North Africa, and Asia. *Viburnum americanum* is native to Canada and the northern United States and is similar to *V. opulus* and *V. roseum.*

In the language of flowers, snowball means thoughts of heaven. "To see the World in a Grain of Sand, and a 0 0 Heaven in a Wild Flower, hold Infinity in the palm of your hand, an eternity in an hour." Wm. Blake o

VERONICA

Sentiment: Fidelity

Whither thou goest, I will go.
Ruth 1:16

The story of Ruth is an apt one to represent fidelity. When Naomi's son, Ruth's husband, died, Naomi decided to return to Bethlehem. When Naomi entreated Ruth to return to her own mother's house, Ruth said, "Entreat me not to leave thee, or to return from following after thee: for whither thou goest, I will go; and where thou lodgest, I will lodge: thy people shall be my people, and thy God my God."

Botanical Name: *Veronica officinalis*
Common Names: common speedwell, fluellen, ground-hele, speedwell, veronica

Some authorities believe this plant was named in honor of St. Veronica; others contend it was derived from the Greek words *phero*, I bring, and *nike*, victory; still others say it is from the Greek word, *beronlike*, meaning faithful likeness. *Officinalis* means that it is medical, recognized in the pharmacopoeia. It is alleged that the plant was called speedwell because the petals fall as soon as the flower is picked.

According to horticulturalist L. H. Bailey, Isaac Anderson-Henry raised the first hybrid veronicas in 1848; his work was continued by others, and many hybrids have this parentage, with *Veronica speciosa* much in evidence. The old herbals indicate that all species of veronica possess a slight degree of astringency; many species were once used in medicine.

Description & Habitat: This low, mat-forming perennial has slender stems, up to eighteen inches long. The oblong green leaves are toothed, one-half to two inches long. May through July, tiny flowers with four petals, about one-fifth-inch wide, form spike-like clusters of pale purple or blue flowers. Native to forests and mountains of Britain, Europe, Asia, and North America, the common speedwell grows under trees and in shady places where no grass will grow. Many hybrid forms of veronica are cultivated as annuals and perennials that thrive in good garden soil in sunny locations.

"...whither thou goest, I will go..." Ruth 1:16

In the language of flowers, veronica-speedwell means fidelity.

VIOLET

Sentiment: Faithfulness or Faith

Now faith is the substance of things hoped for, the evidence of things not seen.
Hebrews 11:1

The peculiar life cycle of violets approximates the meaning of this text from Hebrews. Violets produce flowers in both spring and autumn. In spring, the flowers are fully formed and sweet-scented; they are full of honey and ready for bees, but they bloom ahead of bee time and rarely set seed.   In autumn, the flowers are very small, hidden among the leaves, with no petals and no scent and produce an abundance of seed. They are apt emblems of faith and have also been associated with innocence and modesty.

Botanical Species: *Viola odorata*
Common Names: March violet, sweet violet, sweet-scented violet, violet

Violet is the diminutive of *Viola*, the Latin form of the Greek name *Ione*. Some writers explain this association with a Greek legend in which Jupiter changed his beloved Io into a white heifer and caused violets to grow as food for her. Other writers refer to the Latin word *vias*, meaning wayside, for the derivation of the word *violet*. The flowers are generally deep purple, giving their name to the color that is called after them.

Sweet violets have long been grown for their essential oils. In the nineteenth century especially in the south of France, huge quantities were cultivated for perfume. In 1893 two German scientists discovered the chemical formula of the violet scent, also present in the orris root of the iris, and patented it, calling it "Ionone."

Description & Habitat: The toothed, heart-shaped leaves often roll up when young, forming two tight coils. The flowers are deep violet, occasionally white or pale rose, and fragrant. They have five unequal petals – two oval, above, two lateral with a hairy center line, and a lower petal forming a long hollow spur, rounded at the end. Violets are among the self-fertilizing plants called *cleistogamous*. A native of Europe, Africa, and Asia, the sweet violet has many forms, including doubles, varying in size and color.

In the language of flowers, the blue violet means faithfulness or faith. "Now faith is the substance of things hoped for, the evidence of things not seen." Hebrews 11:1.

WATER LILY

Sentiment: Purity of Heart

Blessed are the pure in heart: for they shall see God.

Matthew 5:8

The text is from the Beatitudes, eight blessings spoken by Jesus in the Sermon on the Mount.

Botanical Species: *Nymphea odorata*
Common Names: sweet-scented water lily, water lily, white pond lily

Nymphea is a water nymph in Greek and Roman mythology. Its meaning in the language of flowers, purity of heart, may relate to the purity of the white petals or to the water nymphs, who were virgins and symbols of purity.

The flowers open as the sun rises and are usually closed by noon. The leaf stalk is soft and spongy and has four main air channels for the movement of oxygen and other gases from the leaves to the root stock buried in the muck. There are about forty species; each species opens and closes at a particular time each day, and each flower opens from one to seven successive days, then sinks into the water where the seed ripens.

Henry David Thoreau wrote in his journal on June 26, 1852, "The *Nymphaea odorata*, water nymph, sweet water-lily, pond-lily, in bloom. A superb flower, our lotus, queen of the waters. Now is the solstice in still waters. How sweet, innocent, wholesome its fragrance! How pure its white petals, though its root is in the mud! It must answer in my mind for what the Orientals say of the lotus flower."

Description & Habitat: The large round or oval leaves are up to a foot in diameter, shiny green on top, reddish beneath; they float or, if crowded, rise above the surface of the water. Shaped like a large rosette, the flowers have four green sepals and many fragrant white or pinkish petals, three to five inches wide, that narrow in width. The petals surround numerous yellow fringe-like filaments or stamen. These aquatic plants, native to ponds and quiet waters in the northeastern United States and parts of Canada, bloom spring through summer.

In the language of flowers, the water lily means purity of heart. "Blessed are the pure in heart: for they shall see God." Matthew 5:8

Susan Loy

ZINNIA

Sentiment: Thoughts of Absent Friends

Friendly thoughts and earnest good wishes thus create and maintain what
is practically a guardian angel, always at the side of the person thought of.

A. E. Powell

I do not know the source of this text, but years ago several of my friends received handwritten copies of it from me when I first discovered these lines. I like the notion that our friendly thoughts can actually protect those we care for.

Botanical species: *Zinnia elegans*
Common Names: youth and old age, zinnia

Linnaeus named the zinnia after Johann Gottfried Zinn, a medical professor at Gottingen University who lived from 1727 to 1759. Zinnias perish slowly without closing their petals or losing their bright tints; on this account they have sometimes been called youth and old age.

Although there were some important introductions of zinnia strains in the second half of the nineteenth century, zinnias were not really improved until the 1900's when, according to the writer Diana Wells, "one flower in a whole field of experimental zinnias, grown by Burpee, was used as the basis for breeding most of the hybrids we know today. It was in the sixty-sixth row and known in the trade as 'Old 66.'" Burpee, of course, refers to W. Atlee Burpee and Company.

Description & Habitat: This erect plant grows up to three feet high with green, oval leaves about one inch wide. In the wild and single forms there generally are two types of flowers present, the inner or "disc" flowers and the outer, "ray" flowers. The so-called double forms are merely those in which the disc flowers have taken on the characteristics of the ray flowers. In the original zinnias, the rays were a dull purple color, but zinnias are now a wide range of color. In the original form, the disk was usually yellow or orange, but is nearly absent in modern double forms. The flowers are two to five inches across and bloom July through October. This native of Mexico is a popular garden subject, commonly grown as an annual.

In the language of flowers, zinnia means thoughts of absent friends, always at the side of the person thought of..." Powell + thus create and maintain what is practically a guardian angel, "Friendly thoughts and earnest good wishes + In the language of flowers, zinnia means thoughts of

Opposite: Susan Loy. *The Language of Garden Flowers*, 1998. Watercolor on paper. 15 1/2 x 15 1/2 inches.

These roses under my window make no reference to former roses or to better ones, they are for what they are; they exist with God to-day. There is no time to them. There is simply the rose; it is perfect in every moment of its existence. Before a leaf-bud has burst, its whole life acts; in the leafless root or in the full-blown flower there is no more; in the leafless root or nothing there is one less. Its nature is satisfied and it satisfies nature in all moments alike. Ralph Waldo Emerson, Self-Reliance

Susan Loy

DICTIONARY

OF

THE AMERICAN LANGUAGE OF FLOWERS

BY FLOWER

A

Abatina ....fickleness

Abecedary ....volubility

Acacia, Rose ....chaste love, platonic love

Acacia, Rose............................friendship

Acacia, Rose or White ....elegance

Acacia, Yellow ....concealed love, secret love

Acanthus................................art, the arts

Acanthus................................artifice, the fine arts

Achimenes Cupreata.............such worth is rare

Adder's Tongue ....deceit

Adonis...................................painful recollections, sad memories

Adonis ....remembrance

Ageratum...............................politeness

Agnus Castus ....coldness, indifference

Agnus Castus...........................to live without

Agrimony...............................gratitude

Agrimony ....thankfulness

Ailantus ....lofty aspirations

Allspice ....compassion

Almond ....despair

Almond, Almond Tree ....heedlessness, thoughtlessness

Almond, Common...................indiscretion

Almond, Common...................stupidity

Almond, Flowering ....hope

Aloe ....acute sorrow or affliction

Aloe ....bitterness

Aloe ....grief

Aloe ....imagination

Aloe ....religious superstition

Alyssum, Sweet ....merit before beauty

Alyssum, Sweet.......................worth beyond beauty

Amaranth ....immortality

Amaranth ....unfading

Amaranth ....affection

Amaryllis...............................beautiful, but timid

Amaryllis................................haughtiness, pride

Amaryllis .... splendid beauty
Amaryllis .... timidity
Ambrosia .... love returned
Amethyst .... admiration
Andromeda .... self-sacrifice
Andromeda .... will you help me?
Anemone .... forsaken
Anemone .... anticipation, expectation
Anemone .... frailty, sickness
Anemone .... withered hopes
Anemone .... your frown I defy
Anemone, Wood .... forlornness
Angelica .... inspiration
Angelica .... magic
Angrec .... royalty
Apple .... temptation
Apple Blossom .... fame speaks you/him great and good
Apple Blossom .... preference
Apricot .... temptation
Apricot Blossom .... doubt
Arbor Vitae .... live for me
Arbor Vitae .... unchanging friendship
Arbor Vitae, American .... immortality
Arbor Vitae, American .... thine till death
Arbutus .... thee only do I love
Arethusa .... fear
Arnica .... let me heal thy grief
Arum .... ardor, zeal
Arum .... deceit and ferocity
Ash, Ash Tree .... grandeur
Asparagus .... emulation
Aspen Tree .... fear
Aspen Tree .... lamentation
Aspen, Aspen Tree .... excessive sensibility
Asphodel .... my regrets follow you to the grave
Asphodel .... remembered beyond the tomb

Aster..afterthought
Aster ....beauty in retirement
Aster ....cheerfulness in old age
Aster ....farewell
Aster ....welcome to a stranger
Aster, China............................love of variety, variety,
                                     variety of charms
Aster, China ....your sentiments meet with a return
Aster, China, Double...............bounty
Aster, China, Double...............I partake your sentiments
Aster, China, Single ....I will think of it
Auricula.................................confidence
Auricula.................................painting
Auricula.................................pride of riches or
                                     newly acquired fortune
Auricula, Scarlet......................avarice
Auricula, Scarlet......................pride
Auricula, Scarlet......................wealth is not happiness
Auricula, Yellow ....splendor
Autumn Crocus ....growing old, I do not fear to grow old
Azalea ....romance
Azalea....................................temperance

B
Bachelor's Button..................celibacy
Bachelor's Button ....I with the morning's love have made sport
Balm......................................pleasantry
Balm ....social intercourse,
                                     sweets of social intercourse
Balm ....sympathy
Balm of Gilead ....cure, I am cured, healing, relief
Balm of Gilead ....sympathetic feeling
Balm, Gentle ....joking
Balm, Gentle ....pleasantry
Balm, Molucca ....you excite my curiosity
Balm, Sweet ....charms
Balsam ....health

Balsam, Balsamine ....impatience
Balsam, Red ....impatient resolve
Balsam, Red ....touch me not
Barberry..................................ill temper, petulance, sour disposition
Barberry..................................sharpness, tartness
Bartonia, Golden ....does he possess riches?
Basil ....good wishes
Basil..hate, hatred
Bayberry...............................I respect thy tears
Bayberry ....instruction
Bayberry ....I will enlighten you
Bearded Crepis ....protection
Bear's-breech ....art
Bee Orchis ....industry
Beech.......................................glory
Beech.......................................lovers' tryst
Beech.......................................wedded love
Beech Tree ....grandeur, prosperity
Begonia ....deformity
Belladonna...............................silence, hush!
Bellflower ....acknowledgement
Bellflower..................................constancy, a constant heart
Bellflower..................................delicate, lonely as this flower
Bellflower..................................gratitude
Bellflower..................................grief
Bellflower..................................submission
Bellflower, Pyramidal ....aspiring
Belvedere ....I declare against you
Betony.....................................surprise
Bilberry ....treachery
Birch ....elegance, gracefulness
Birch ....meekness
Blackthorn...............................difficulty
Bladdernut ....amusement, frivolity, frivolous amusement
Bladdernut ....trifling character, a trifling character
Bluebell...................................sorrowful regret

67

Borage......................................	abruptness, bluntness, rudeness
Borage	roughness of manner
Bouncing Bess	intrusion
Box	constancy
Box	stoicism
Bramble	envy
Bramble	lowliness
Bramble	remorse
Broom	anger
Broom...................................	ardor
Broom...................................	humility
Broom...................................	mirth
Broom...................................	neatness
Browallia	can you bear poverty?
Bryony	prosperity
Buckbean...............................	calm, calmness, calm repose, repose
Buckbean................................	flatterer's smile
Bugloss..................................	falsehood
Bugloss..................................	hypocrisy
Bulrush	docility
Bulrush	indecision
Bulrush	indiscretion
Burdock.................................	importunity
Burdock	proximity undesirable
Burdock	touch me not
Burr	you worry me
Buttercup...............................	childishness
Buttercup	distrust
Buttercup	ingratitude
Buttercup	memories of childhood
Buttercup	riches, desire of riches, I wish I was rich, wealth
Buttercup	you are radiant with charms, you are rich in attractions
Butterfly Weed	cure for the heartache
Butterfly Weed.........................	let me go
Butterfly Weed.........................	medicine

68

C
Cabbage..................................gain, profit
Cacalia...................................adulation
Cactus ....ardent love
Cactus, Common ....I burn
Cactus, Serpentine..................horror
Cactus, Snake ....you terrify me
Calceolaria ....I offer you pecuniary assistance,
                        I offer you my fortune
Calceolaria.............................novelty
Calla.....................................feminine modesty
Calla ....magnificent beauty
Calla ....modesty
Calla Lily...............................feminine beauty
Calycanthus...........................benevolence
Calycanthus ....compassion
Camellia...............................my destiny is in your hands
Camellia ....perfect loveliness
Camellia Japonica ....modest merit
Camellia Japonica ....supreme loveliness
Camellia Japonica ....unpretending excellence
Camphire..............................fragrance
Campion, Rose ....love's messenger
Campion, Rose ....only deserve my love
Campion, Rose ....you are without pretension
Candytuft ....architecture
Candytuft................................indifference
Cardamine............................infatuation
Cardamine ....paternal error
Cardinal Flower ....distinction
Cardinal Flower.......................preferment
Carnation ....pride and beauty
Carnation, Deep Red ....alas! for my poor heart
Carnation, Striped ....refusal
Catalpa Tree ....beware of the coquette

Catchfly ....artifice
Catchfly ....pretended love
Catchfly ....snare, a snare
Catchfly ....youthful love
Catchfly, White ....betrayed
Cattleya ....mature charms
Cattleya, Pineli ....matronly grace
Cedar ....I think of thee
Cedar ....spiritual strength
Cedar ....protection
Cedar ....strength
Cedar ....think of me
Cedar Leaf.............................I live for thee
Cedar of Lebanon....................incorruptible
Celandine...............................deceptive hopes
Celandine................................future happiness
Celandine................................joys to come
Cereus, Creeping ....horror
Cereus, Creeping....................modest genius
Cereus, Night-blooming...........transient beauty
Chamomile ....energy in adversity
Chamomile ....mercy
Cherry, Bird ....hope
Cherry Blossom.......................spiritual beauty
Cherry, Cherry Tree ....education, good education
Cherry Tree, White ....deception
Chervil, Garden ....sincerity
Chestnut ....deceptive appearances
Chestnut Tree ....do me justice, render me justice
Chestnut, Chestnut Tree..........luxury
Chickweed ....rendezvous
Chickweed................................star of my existence
Chickweed, Mouse-eared.........ingenuous simplicity
Chicory ....frugality, prudent economy
Chorozema Varium................you have many lovers
Christmas Rose......................relieve my anxiety

Chrysanthemum .... slighted affections
Chrysanthemum, Chinese .... cheerfulness under adversity
Chrysanthemum, Chinese .... loveliness and cheerfulness
Chrysanthemum, Red .... I love
Chrysanthemum, White .... truth
Chrysanthemum, Yellow .... a heart left to desolation
Chrysanthemum, Yellow .... slighted love
Cineraria .... always delightful
Cinquefoil .... love, constant, but hopeless
Cinquefoil .... maternal affection
Cinquefoil .... parental love
Cistus .... popular favor
Cistus, Gum .... I shall die tomorrow
Citron .... estrangement
Citron .... ill-natured beauty
Citron .... marriage
Clarkia .... the variety of your conversation delights me
Clematis .... artifice
Clematis .... filial affection, filial love
Clematis .... mental beauty/excellence
Clematis .... safety
Clematis, English .... traveler's joy
Clematis, Evergreen .... poverty
Clianthus .... self-seeking
Clianthus .... worldliness
Clotbur .... detraction
Clotbur .... rudeness
Clove .... dignity
Clover .... I promise
Clover .... industry
Clover .... providence, provident
Clover .... revenge
Clover, Four-leaved .... be mine
Clover, White .... lightheartedness
Clover, White .... promise
Clover, White .... think of me

Cobaea	gossip
Cockscomb	foppery
Cockscomb	singularity
Coltsfoot	justice shall be done to you, justice to you
Coltsfoot	maternal care
Columbine	desertion
Columbine	folly
Columbine	I cannot give thee up
Columbine, Purple	resolved to win
Columbine, Red	anxious, trembling
Convolvulus	bonds
Convolvulus	dangerous insinuation
Convolvulus	humility
Convolvulus	importunity
Convolvulus	insinuation
Convolvulus	night
Convolvulus	obstinacy
Convolvulus	uncertainty
Convolvulus	worth sustained by affections
Convolvulus, Field	captivation
Convolvulus Major	extinguished hopes
Corchorus	impatience, impatient of absence
Coreopsis	always cheerful
Coreopsis	happy at all times
Coreopsis	love at first sight
Coriander	concealed merit, hidden merit or worth
Coriander	merit
Corn	abundance, plenty, riches
Corn, Broken	quarrel
Corn Cockle	gentility
Corn Cockle	worth above beauty
Corn Flower	delicacy
Corn Flower	single blessedness
Corn Straw	agreement
Coronella, Coronilla	success crown your wishes
Cosmelia Subra	the charm of a blush
Cotton Plant	greatness

Cowslip ....native grace, winning grace
Cowslip....................................pensiveness
Cowslip....................................youthful beauty
Cowslip, American..................divine beauty
Cowslip, American..................you are my divinity
Crab Blossom..........................ill nature
Crab Blossom, Siberian...........deeply interesting
Cranberry ....cure for heartache
Cranberry................................hardihood, hardiness
Crape Myrtle ....eloquence
Cress ....power
Cress ....stability
Crocus....................................abuse not
Crocus....................................cheerfulness
Crocus....................................mirth
Crocus....................................patience
Crocus....................................smiles
Crocus....................................youth, youthful gladness
Cross of Jerusalem ....devotion
Crowfoot, Aconite-leaved ....luster
Crown Imperial ....imperial power, power
Crown Imperial ....majesty
Crown Imperial ....pride of birth, pride of riches
Crowsbill ....envy
Cucumber..............................criticism
Cudweed ....never-ceasing/unceasing remembrance
Cuphea....................................impatience
Currant....................................thy frown will kill me
Currant, Branch of....................you please all
Cyclamen................................diffidence
Cypress ....death
Cypress ....despair
Cypress ....disappointed hopes
Cypress ....mourning
Cypress ....sorrow
Cypress Tree............................death and eternal sorrow

D
Daffodil ....chivalry
Daffodil ....deceitful hope
Daffodil ....regard
Daffodil ....uncertainty
Daffodil ....unrequited love
Dahlia....................................dignity
Dahlia ....elegance and dignity
Dahlia ....forever thine
Dahlia ....heartless beauty
Dahlia ....instability
Dahlia ....pomp
Daisy ....innocence, innocence and
                                            beauty, innocence and hope
Daisy, Double..........................participation
Daisy, Garden..........................I reciprocate/share your sentiments
Daisy, Ox-eye..........................token, a token
Daisy, Parti-colored.................beauty
Daisy, Wild or White ....I will think of it
Dandelion ....coquetry
Dandelion ....depart
Dandelion ....oracle, rustic oracle, love's oracle
Dandelion ....youthful recollections
Daphne..................................coquetry
Daphne ....desire to please, I desire to please
Daphne ....glory
Daphne ....immortality
Daphne ....love in a snow wreath
Daphne ....sweets to the sweet
Daphne ....timidity
Daphne Odora ....painting the lily
Darnel ....vice
Datura...................................deceitful charms
Datura ....disguise
Datura ....I dreamed of thee
Day Lily ....coquetry
Dew Plant ....serenade, a serenade

Dianthus ....make haste
Diosma ....your single elegance charms me
Dipladenia Crassinoda...........you are too bold
Dipteracanthus Spectablis .....fortitude
Dittany ....childbirth
Dittany of Crete.......................birth
Dittany of Crete, White...........passion
Dock ....patience
Dodder ....baseness, meanness
Dogsbane ....deceit, falsehood
Dogwood ....durability, duration
Dogwood ....honesty
Dogwood ....love undiminished by adversity
Dogwood ....true nobility
Dragon Plant..........................snare
Dragon's Claw ....danger
Dragonwort ....horror
Dutchman's Pipe...................prodigality
Dwarf Pink............................innocence
Dyer's Broom ....neatness
Dyer's Weed ....design

E
Ebenaster...............................night
Ebony.....................................blackness
Ebony ....hypocrisy
Echites Atropurpurea ....be warned in time
Eglantine ....I wound to heal
Eglantine..................................poetry
Eglantine, American................imagination
Eglantine, American................simplicity
Elder ....compassion
Elder ....zeal, zealousness
Elm..dignity
Elm, American ....patriotism
Enchanter's Nightshade.........fascination
Enchanter's Nightshade ....sorcery, witchcraft

Enchanter's Nightshade ....spell
Endive.....................................frugality
Endive.....................................medicine
Entoca.....................................gift, a gift
Escallonia ....opinion
Eschscholtzia.........................do not refuse me
Eternal Flower ....eternity
Eupatorium ....delay
Euphorbia ....reproof
Evening Primrose..................I am more faithful than thou
Evening Primrose ....inconstancy
Evening Primrose ....silent love
Evergreen ....poverty, poverty and worth
Evergreen Thorn......................solace in adversity
Everlasting ....always remembered,
                                 never-ceasing remembrance
Eyebright................................your eyes are bewitching

F
False Dragon Head................bravery
Fennel ....strength
Fennel ....worthy of praise, worthy all praise
Fern.......................................fascination
Fern.......................................magic
Fern.......................................sincerity
Fern, Flowering ....reverie
Fern, Maidenhair ....discretion
Fern, Maidenhair ....secrecy
Fern, Walking..........................curiosity
Feverfew ....beneficence
Fig ....argument
Fig..longevity
Fig Tree ....prolific, profuseness
Flax ....domestic industry
Flax..fate

Flax..I am sensible of your kindness,
                                      I feel your kindness

Flax, Dried...............................utility

Flora's Bells ....you are without pretension

Fool's Parsley ....silliness

Forget Me Not.........................forget me not

Forget Me Not ....true love

Four-o'clock ....time

Four-o'clock.............................timidity

Foxglove.................................delirium

Foxglove.................................I am not ambitious for myself,
                                      but for you

Foxglove.................................I am not changed

Foxglove.................................insincerity

Foxglove.................................south

Foxglove.................................stateliness

Franciscea Latifolia...............beware of false friends

Frankincense.........................the incense of a faithful heart

Fraxinella ....fire

Fritillaria ....persecution

Fuchsia...................................grace

Fuchsia ....humble love

Fuchsia, Globe-flowered ....confiding love

Fuchsia, Scarlet ....taste

Fumitory.................................spleen

G

Gardenia.................................refinement

Gentian ....I love you best when you are sad

Gentian ....intrinsic worth

Gentian ....virgin pride

Gentian, Yellow ....ingratitude

Geranium ....confidence

Geranium................................deceit

Geranium................................gentility

Geranium, Dark.......................melancholy

Geranium, Ivy ....bridal favor
Geranium, Lemon ....serenity, tranquility of mind
Geranium, Lemon ....unexpected meeting
Geranium, Mourning...............despondency
Geranium, Nutmeg..................expected meeting
Geranium, Oak ....true friendship
Geranium, Penciled-leaf..........ingenuity
Geranium, Rose-scented ....preference
Geranium, Scarlet...................consolation, comforting
Geranium, Scarlet...................folly, stupidity
Geranium, Scarlet...................preference
Geranium, Scarlet...................thou art changed
Geranium, Silver-leaved ....recall
Geranium, Sorrowful...............melancholy mind/spirit
Geranium, Wild.......................steadfast piety
Gladiolus ....ready armed
Gladiolus ....strength of character
Glasswort...............................pretension
Globe Amaranth....................hope in misery
Globe Amaranth ....I change not, unchangeable
Globe Amaranth ....immortality
Glory Flower...........................glorious beauty
Goat's Rue...............................reason
Golden Locks, Flax-leaved .....tardiness
Golden Rod ....encouragement
Golden Rod ....precaution
Gooseberry.............................anticipation
Goosefoot ....goodness
Goosefoot, Grass-leaved ....I declare war against you
Gorse.......................................cheerfulness in adversity
Gourd......................................bulk, bulkiness, extent
Grammanthes Chloraflora....your temper is too hasty
Grape......................................charity
Grape, Wild.............................mirth
Grass.......................................submission
Grass.......................................usefulness, utility

78

Grass, Canary ....perseverance
Grass, Foxtail ....sporting
Grass, Vernal.........................poor but happy,
                            we may be poor, but we will be happy
Ground Ivy.............................enjoyment
Ground Pine.........................complaint
Groundsel Tree......................intoxication
Gum Tree...............................enthusiasm

H
Hackmetack ....single blessedness
Hand Flower Tree ....warning
Hawkweed ....quick-sightedness
Hawthorn ....hope
Hazel ....peace
Hazel..reconciliation
Heather ....solitude, solitude is sometimes the best society
Helenium ....tears
Heliotrope.............................devotion, devoted attachment
Heliotrope................................I turn to thee
Heliotrope................................infatuation, I love you
Heliotrope................................intoxication, intoxicated with pleasure
Hellebore ....calumny
Hellebore ....scandal
Hemlock..................................you will be/cause my death
Hemp ....fate
Henbane..................................defect, fault, imperfection
Hepatica..................................confidence
Hibiscus ....beauty is vain
Hibiscus...................................delicate beauty
Hibiscus...................................trifling beauty
Hickory ....glory
Hoarhound ....frozen kindness
Hoarhound, Black ....I reject you
Holly..domestic happiness
Holly..foresight

Hollyhock ....ambition
Hollyhock ....fruitfulness, fecundity
Honesty ....fascination
Honesty...................................forgetfulness
Honesty...................................honesty
Honey Flower.........................love sweet and secret,
                my love is sweet and secret
Honeysuckle ....bonds of love
Honeysuckle ....devoted love,
                generous and devoted affection
Honeysuckle ....fidelity
Honeysuckle ....fraternal love
Honeysuckle, Coral ....the color of my fate
Honeysuckle, French...............rustic beauty
Honeysuckle, Trumpet ....I have dreamed of thee
Honeysuckle, Wild...................inconstancy
Hops ....injustice
Hornbeam ....ornament
Horse Chestnut.....................luxury, luxuriancy
Houseleek ....domestic industry
Houseleek ....vivacity
Houstonia ....content, contentment, quiet happiness
Hoya..sculpture
Hoyabella...............................contentment
Humbleplant ....despondency
Hyacinth ....come, play
Hyacinth ....constancy
Hyacinth ....game, play, sport
Hyacinth ....grief, sorrow, sorrowful, I am sorry
Hyacinth ....jealousy
Hyacinth, White ....unobtrusive loveliness
Hydrangea..............................boaster
Hydrangea ....heartlessness
Hydrangea ....you are cold
Hyssop ....cleanliness
Hyssop...................................purification

I

Ice Plant	an old beau
Ice Plant	formality
Ice Plant	your looks freeze me, you freeze me
Imbricaria	uprightness, sentiments of honor
Indian Cress	resignation
Indian Cress	warlike trophy
Indian Mallow	estimation
Ipomoea	attachment, I attach myself to you
Ipomoea	busybody
Ipomopsis	suspense
Iris	fire, I burn
Iris	message, I have a message for thee
Iris	my compliments
Iris, Flame, Yellow	flame, flame of love, passion
Ivy	fidelity
Ivy	friendship, lasting friendship
Ivy	I have found one true heart
Ivy	wedded love, marriage, matrimony
Ivy, Sprig of, with Tendrils	assiduous to please

J

Jacob's Ladder	come down, come down to me
Jasmine	amiableness, amiability
Jasmine, Cape	I'm too happy, transport of joy
Jasmine, Carolina	separation
Jasmine, Indian	I attach myself to you
Jasmine, Spanish	sensuality
Jasmine, Yellow	grace and elegance
Jessamine, Virginian	soul of my soul
Jonquil	affection returned
Jonquil	desire
Jonquil	I desire a return of affection
Joy	friendship

81

Judas Flower, Judas Tree......unbelief
Judas Tree................................betrayal
Julienne, White......................despair not; God is everywhere
Juniper, Juniper Berries..........asylum, protection, succor
Justicia................................female loveliness,
                  perfection of female loveliness

K
Kennedia, Kennedya..............mental beauty
King-Cup................................desire of riches, riches

L
Laburnum.............................forsaken
Laburnum................................pensive beauty
Lady's Slipper......................capricious beauty
Lady's Slipper..........................fickleness
Lady's Slipper..........................win me and wear me
Lake Flower..........................retirement
Lantana................................rigor
Lapageria Rosea....................there is no unalloyed good
Larch..................................audacity
Larch......................................boldness
Larkspur..............................ardent attachment
Larkspur.................................fickleness, inconstancy
Larkspur.................................haughtiness
Larkspur.................................levity, lightness
Laurel..................................glory
Laurel.....................................I change but in dying
Laurel.....................................love's memory, love and memory
Laurel.....................................reward of merit
Laurel.....................................virtue is true beauty,
                 virtue makes her charming
Laurel, Ground........................perseverance
Laurel in Flower.......................perfidity
Laurel, Mountain.....................ambition
Laurestina, Laurustinus..........token, a token
Laurestina, Laurustinus...........I die if neglected

Lavender ....acknowledgement
Lavender..................................assiduity
Lavender..................................confession
Lavender..................................mistrust, distrust
Leaf, Leaves ....sadness, sorrow
Leaf, Walking..........................how came you here?
Leaves, Autumnal or Dead.......melancholy
Lemon..................................zest
Lemon Blossom ....fidelity in love
Lemon, Lemon Blossom ....discretion
Leschenaultia Splendens........you are charming
Lettuce ....cold-hearted, coldness
Lichen ....dejection
Lichen..................................solitude
Licorice, Wild.......................I declare against you
Lilac ....first emotion of love,
                                                    awakening love
Lilac..................................forsaken
Lilac, Field ....humility
Lilac, Field or Purple ....fastidiousness
Lilac, White...........................joy of worth
Lilac, White...........................youth, youthful innocence
Lily ....majesty
Lily ....purity
Lily ....purity and beauty
Lily ....purity and modesty
Lily ....purity and sweetness
Lily, Japanese........................you cannot deceive me
Lily, Scarlet...........................high souled
Lily, Superb...........................splendor
Lily, Yellow ....coquetry
Lily, Yellow ....falsehood
Lily, Yellow ....gaiety, playful gaiety
Lily of the Valley ....delicate simplicity
Lily of the Valley ....the heart withering in secret
Lily of the Valley ....return of happiness
Lily of the Valley ....unconscious sweetness

Linden, American....................matrimony
Linden or Lime Tree ....conjugal love, conjugal fidelity
Lint...I feel my obligations
Loasa......................................pleasure
Lobelia ....arrogance
Lobelia....................................splendor
Lobelia....................................malevolence
Locust ....affection beyond the grave
Locust ....vicissitude
Locust Tree...........................elegance
London Pride ....frivolity
Lophospermum......................ecstasy
Lote Tree ....concord
Love in a Puzzle....................embarrassment
Love-in-a-Mist ....artifice
Love-in-a-Mist ....you puzzle me, perplexity
Love-Lies-Bleeding................hopeless, not heartless
Lucern ....agriculture
Lucern.....................................life
Lupine....................................dejection, sorrow
Lupine.....................................voraciousness
Lychnis ....ever till now
Lychnis ....hope in love
Lychnis ....religious enthusiasm, a religious enthusiast
Lychnis, Meadow ....wit
Lychnis, Scarlet.......................sun-beamed eyes

M
Madder ....calumny
Madwort, **Rock** ....tranquility
Magnolia................................love of nature
Magnolia..................................magnificence
Magnolia..................................peerless and proud
Magnolia, Laurel-leaved ....dignity, high-souled
Magnolia, Swamp ....perseverance
Mallow ....goodness
Mallow ....mildness

84

Mallow, Marsh ....humanity
Mallow, Marsh ....beneficence, mild or sweet disposition
Mallow, Syrian ....consumed by love
Mallow, Syrian ....persuasion
Malon Creeana ....will you share my fortunes?
Manchineel Tree..................falsehood
Mandrake...............................horror
Mandrake..................................rarity
Manrandia............................courtesy
Maple ....reserve
Maple..retirement
Maple, Rock ....rescue
Marianthus............................hope for better days
Marigold ....chagrin, pain
Marigold ....contempt
Marigold ....cruelty
Marigold ....grief
Marigold ....inquietude
Marigold, African....................vulgar minds, vulgar-minded
Marigold and Cypress ....despair
Marigold, French....................jealousy
Marigold, Garden ....uneasiness
Marigold, Prophetic.................prediction
Marigold, Small Cape ....omen, presage
Marigold, Yellow ....sacred affections
Marjoram...............................blushes
Marsh Andromeda ....bound by fate
Mayweed ....rumor
Meadow Saffron ....growing old, I do not fear to grow old
Meadow Saffron......................my best/happiest days are gone
Meadowsweet.........................praise
Meadowsweet...........................uselessness
Melilot....................................philanthropy
Mercury................................goodness
Mermaid Weed ....necessity
Mesembryanthemum ....idleness
Mignonette ....moral and intellectual beauty

Mignonette ....your qualities surpass your charms,
　　　　　　　　　　　　　　　your qualities surpass your loveliness
Milkvetch...............................your presence softens my pain
Milkweed ....conquer your love
Milkwort................................hermitage
Mimosa ....sensibility, sensitiveness
Mint ....virtue
Mistletoe ....parasite
Mistletoe.................................I rise above all, I surmount
　　　　　　　　　　　　　　　all obstacles, obstacles to
　　　　　　　　　　　　　　　be overcome
Mitraria Coccinea ....dullness, indolence
Mock Orange ....counterfeit
Monarda.................................I value your sympathy
Monarda Amplexicaulis ....your whims are quite unbearable
Monkshood.............................a deadly foe is near
Monkshood...............................chivalry, knight errantry
Monkshood...............................deceit
Monkshood...............................misanthropy
Morning Glory.......................affection
Morning Glory ....repose
Moss ....affection
Moss ....ennui
Moss ....maternal love
Moss, English ....fortitude
Moss, Ice/Iceland ....health
Motherwort ....concealed love, secret love
Mountain Ash ....prudence
Mountain Ash..........................talisman
Mountain Ash..........................with me you are safe
Mourning Bride.....................I have lost all
Moving Plant.........................agitation
Mudwort................................tranquility
Mudwort, Mugwort ....happiness
Mulberry Tree, Black ....I shall not survive you
Mulberry Tree, Red, White......wisdom

Mullein......................................good nature
Mushroom ....I can't entirely trust you, suspicion
Musk Plant............................meeting, a meeting
Musk Plant ....weakness
Mustard, Mustard Seed...........indifference
Myrobalan............................privation
Myrrh ....gladness
Myrtle ....love, love in absence

N
Narcissus ....egotism
Narcissus ....self-love, self-esteem
Narcissus, False.......................delusive hope
Nasturtium ....heroism
Nasturtium ....patriotism
Nasturtium ....splendor
Nemophila ....prosperity
Nemophila ....success everywhere
Nettle......................................cruelty
Nettle ....slander
Nettle ....you are spiteful
Nettle, Nettle Tree...................conceit
Nightshade............................dark thoughts
Nightshade...............................death
Nightshade...............................falsehood
Nightshade...............................skepticism
Nightshade...............................truth
Nosegay...................................gallantry

O
Oak..honor
Oak Leaf....................................bravery
Oak Leaf....................................humanity
Oak, Live...................................liberty
Oak, Oak Tree ....hospitality
Oak, White ....independence

Oats...country life
Oats...music, the witching soul of music
Oleander...................................beware, beware!
Oleaster ....providence
Olive...peace
Ophrys, Bee.............................error
Ophrys, Butterfly.....................gaiety
Ophrys, Frog ....disgust
Ophrys, Spider.........................skill
Orange Blossom.....................woman's worth
Orange Blossom ....your purity equals your loveliness
Orange Flowers ....bridal festivities
Orange, Orange Flowers ....chastity
Orange Tree..............................generosity
Orchis ....belle, a belle
Orchis ....error
Orchis, Bee ....industry
Orchis, Butterfly.....................gaiety
Orchis, Spider..........................adroitness, skill
Osier..frankness
Osmunda ....dreams, reverie
Ox Eye, Ox Eye Daisy...........obstacle
Ox Eye, Ox Eye Daisy.............patience

P
Palm..victory
Pansy..love in idleness
Pansy ....tender and pleasant thoughts
Pansy ....think of me
Pansy ....thoughts
Pansy ....you occupy my thoughts
Parsley ....banquet, entertainment, feast, festivity
Parsley ....to win
Pasque Flower.......................you are without pretension,
                                             you have no claims
Passion Flower ....faith
Passion Flower ....holy love

Passion Flower ....passionate love
Passion Flower ....religious fervor/superstition
Pea..appointed meeting
Pea ....lasting pleasure
Pea, Everlasting......................wilt thou go? wilt thou go away?
                                        wilt thou go with me?
Pea, Sweet ....delicate pleasure
Pea, Sweet ....departure
Peach......................................your qualities, like your charms,
                                        are unequaled
Peach Blossom ....I am your captive
Peach Blossom ....this heart is thine
Pear..affection
Pear Tree ....comfort
Pennyroyal ....flee away
Penstemon ....high-bred
Peony ....anger
Peony.......................................bashful shame, shame
Peony.......................................bashfulness
Peony.......................................ostentation
Pepper Plant ....satire
Peppermint............................cordiality, warmth of feeling or
                                        sentiment, warmth
Periwinkle................................early friendship,
                                        early and sincere friendship
Periwinkle................................pleasant/tender recollections,
                                        pleasures of memory
Persicaria...............................restoration
Persimmon ....amid nature's beauties
Persimmon...............................bury me amid nature's beauties
Petunia...................................keep your promises
Petunia.....................................thou art less proud than they deem thee
Petunia.....................................your presence soothes me
Phaseolus ....opportunity
Phlox ....our souls are united
Phlox..unanimity

Pigeon Berry ....indifference
Pimpernel ....change
Pimpernel ....mirth
Pimpernel ....rendezvous, assignation
Pine ....elevation
Pine....................................faith
Pine....................................philosophy
Pine....................................pity
Pine....................................time
Pine, Spruce....................farewell
Pine, Spruce....................hope in adversity
Pineapple ....perfection, you are perfect
Pink ....boldness
Pink..................................contempt, disdain
Pink..................................lively and pure love/affection,
　　　　　　　　　　　　pure and ardent love, pure love
Pink..................................pride, pride and beauty
Pink, China/Indian ....aversion
Pink, Double Indian ....always lovely, you will always be lovely
Pink, Double Red or Red ....woman's love
Pink, Mountain ....aspiring, you are aspiring
Pink, Striped ....refusal
Pink, White............................ingeniousness
Pink, White............................lovely and pure affection
Pink, White............................talent
Pink, White or Variegated........you are fair and fascinating
Pitcher Plant ....instinct
Plane Tree ....genius
Plantain ....white man's footsteps
Plum Tree.............................fidelity
Plum Tree ....keep your promises
Plum Tree, Wild.....................independence
Plumbago............................dignity and meekness
Plumbago Larpenta ....holy wishes
Poinsettia ....brilliancy
Polyanthus, Crimson..............the heart's mystery
Pomegranate ....foolishness, foppishness, fatuity

Pomegranate ....lightning
Pomegranate Flower.................mature elegance
Poor Robin ....compensation or an equivalent
Poplar, Black ....affliction
Poplar, Black ....courage
Poplar, White............................time
Poppy ....consolation, consolation of sleep,
                                consolation to the sick
Poppy...fantastic extravagance
Poppy...forgetfulness
Poppy...oblivion
Poppy...sleep of the heart
Poppy, Red ....evanescent pleasure
Poppy, White.............................my bane, my antidote
Portulaca ....variety
Potato......................................beneficence, benevolence
Potentilla ....beloved daughter
Potentilla...................................I claim, at least, your esteem
Prickly Pear ....satire
Pride of China.........................discussion
Pride of China ....dissension
Primrose ....childhood
Primrose ....early youth, youth
Primrose ....have confidence in me
Primrose ....modest worth
Primrose ....sadness
Primrose ....unpatronized merit
Primrose, Chinese ....lasting love
Privet ....defense, protection
Privet ....prohibition
Pyrus Japonica ....fairies' fire

Q
Quamoclit................................busybody
Queen of the Prairie..............nobility
Queen's Rocket......................you are the queen of coquettes
Quince....................................allurement, temptation

R
Raspberry...............................remorse
Reed ....complaisance
Reed...indiscretion
Reed...music
Reed, Flowering ....confidence in heaven
Rest Harrow.........................obstacle
Rest Harrow ....patience
Rhododendron ....beware
Rhododendron ....danger
Rhododendron ....talking
Rhodora................................beauty in retirement
Rhubarb ....advice
Rocket...................................fashion, fashionable
Rocket......................................rivalry
Rocket......................................you are the queen of coquettes
Rose......................................beauty
Rose ....home
Rose ....I wound to heal
Rose ....love
Rose, Austrian ....loveliness, thou art all that is
        lovely, thou art very lovely
Rose, Bridal............................happy love
Rose, Burgundy.......................simplicity and beauty, unconscious beauty
Rose, Cabbage........................ambassador of love
Rose, Carolina ....love is dangerous
Rose, China ....beauty always/ever new
Rose, China/Multiflora.............charms, many charms
Rose, China/Multiflora.............grace
Rose, China, Dark ....forsaken
Rose, Christmas.......................tranquilize my anxiety
Rose, Daily ....lightness
Rose, Daily ....thy smile I aspire to
Rose, Damask..........................bashful love
Rose, Damask..........................blushing beauty
Rose, Damask..........................brilliant complexion,
        freshness of complexion

Rose, Damask...........................youth
Rose, Dog................................love, pleasure and pain
Rose, Dog................................pleasure and pain
Rose, Dog................................simplicity
Rose, Dried White...................death preferable to loss of innocence
Rose, Full-blown......................secrecy
Rose, Hundred-leaved..............dignity of mind
Rose, Hundred-leaved..............grace, the graces
Rose, Hundred-leaved..............pride
Rose in a Tuft of Grass............there is every thing to be gained
                              by good company
Rose, Japan.............................beauty is your only attraction
Rose Leaf ....I will not trouble you
Rose Leaf ....you may hope
Rose, Maiden-blush.................if you love me, you will find
                              it out
Rose, May ....precocity
Rose, Moss ....love
Rose, Moss ....pleasure without alloy
Rose, Moss ....superior merit
Rose, Moss ....voluptuous love, voluptuousness
Rose Mundi ....variety
Rose Mundi ....you are merry
Rose, Musk..............................capricious beauty
Rose, Musk..............................charming, charms of home
Rose, Pompon ....genteel, gentility
Rose, Pompon ....kindness
Rose, Pompon ....loveliness, pretty, prettiness
Rose, Red-leaved.....................beauty and prosperity
Rose, Red-leaved.....................diffidence
Rose, Single.............................simplicity
Rose, Thornless ....early attachment
Rose, Thornless ....ingratitude
Rose, Unique ....call me not beautiful
Rose, White ....I am worthy of you
Rose, White ....sadness

Rose, White ....secrecy
Rose, White ....silence
Rose, White ....too young to love
Rose, White and Red...............unity
Rose, White with Red ....fire or warmth of the heart
Rose, Wild...............................simplicity
Rose, Withered........................fleeting beauty
Rose, Withered White ....I am in despair
Rose, Withered White ....transient impressions
Rose, Yellow ....infidelity, unfaithfulness
Rose, Yellow ....jealousy
Rose, Yellow ....let us forget
Rose, Yellow Sweetbriar..........decrease of love
Rose, York and Lancaster ....war
Rosebud...................................confession, confession of love
Rosebud...................................young girl, you are young and
                                         beautiful, youthful charms
Rosebud, Red ....pure and lovely, may you ever
                                         be pure and lovely
Rosebud, White ....girlhood
Rosebud, White ....heart unacquainted with love,
                                         the heart that knows not love
Rosebud, White ....too young to love
Roses, Crown of ....reward of merit or virtue
Rosemary...............................fidelity
Rosemary.................................remembrance
Rosemary.................................your presence revives me
Rubus, Rose-leaved.................threats
Rudbeckia ....justice
Rue ....disdain
Rue ....grace
Rue ....purification
Rue ....repentance
Rue, Wild ....manners, morals
Rye Grass ....changeable disposition

S

Saffron	marriage
Saffron Flower	do not abuse
Saffron Flower	excess is dangerous, beware of excess
Sage	domestic virtue
Sage	esteem
Sainfoin	agitation
Saint John's Wort	animosity
Saint John's Wort	superstition
Saint John's Wort	superstitious sanctity
Salvia	energy
Salvia, Blue	wisdom
Sardonia, Sardony	irony
Sarsaparilla	experience
Sassafras	favor
Scabious	unfortunate attachment
Scabious, Sweet	widowhood
Schinus	religious enthusiasm
Sensitive Plant	bashful modesty, bashfulness, modesty
Sensitive Plant	chastity
Sensitive Plant	delicate feelings
Senvy	indifference
Service Tree	prudence
Sidesaddle Flower	will you pledge me?
Shepherd's Purse	I offer you my all
Snakesfoot	horror
Snapdragon	no
Snapdragon	presumption
Snapdragon	you are dazzling, but dangerous
Snowball	age
Snowball	bound
Snowball	thoughts of heaven
Snowball	winter
Snowdrop	consolation
Snowdrop	friend in need, friendship in adversity
Snowdrop	hope

Snowdrop ....I am not a summer friend
Snowdrop Tree ....exhilaration
Sorghum ....labor
Sorrel ....affection
Sorrel ....wit, wit ill-timed
Sorrel, Wild ....parental affection
Sorrel, Wood ....joy
Sorrel, Wood ....maternal tenderness
Southernwood ....bantering, jest, jesting
Spearmint ....warmth of sentiment
Speedwell ....female fidelity
Speedwell ....fidelity
Speedwell, Germander ....facility
Speedwell, Spiked ....resemblance, semblance
Spiderwort ....esteem, not love
Spiderwort ....momentary/transient happiness
Spikenard ....benefits
Spindle Tree ....your image is/charms are
                                    engraven on my heart
Squirting Cucumber ....critic
Stapelia ....offense
Star Flower ....reciprocity
Star of Bethlehem ....follow me
Star of Bethlehem...................guidance
Star of Bethlehem...................the light of our path
Star of Bethlehem...................purity
Star of Bethlehem...................reconciliation
Statice ....sympathy
Stephanotis ....will you accompany me to the East?
Stock, Ten-week ....promptness, promptitude
Stonecrop ....tranquility
Straw, Broken.......................dissension
Straw, Broken.........................rupture, rupture of a contract
Straw, Whole..........................union
Strawberry ....perfect excellence/goodness, perfection
Strawberry Blossom ....foresight
Strawberry Tree......................esteem and love

Strawberry Tree........................perseverance
Sultan, Lilac ....I forgive you
Sultan, White............................sweetness
Sultan, Yellow........................contempt
Sumac ....splendid misery
Sumac ....splendor
Sumac, Venice........................intellectual excellence
Summer Savory ....success
Sunflower ....false riches
Sunflower ....lofty thoughts, lofty and pure thoughts
Sunflower ....smile on me still
Sunflower, Dwarf....................adoration, your devout adorer
Sunflower, Tall........................haughtiness
Sweet Flag ....fitness
Sweet Potato...........................hidden qualities
Sweet Sultan...........................congratulations
Sweet Sultan............................felicity, happiness
Sweet William ....childhood
Sweet William ....craftiness
Sweet William ....dexterity
Sweet William ....finesse
Sweet William ....gallantry
Sweet William ....smile, a smile
Sweet William ....stratagem
Sycamore ....curiosity
Sycamore ....woodland beauty
Syringa...................................counterfeit
Syringa ....disappointment
Syringa ....fraternal affection, love or sympathy
Syringa ....memory

T
Tamarisk ....crime
Tansy ....resistance
Tansy, Wild ....I declare war against you
Teasel ....misanthropy
Teasel, Fuller's.........................austerity

Tendrils ....ties
Thistle ....austerity
Thistle.......................................importunity
Thistle.......................................independence
Thistle.......................................misanthropy
Thistle.......................................never forget
Thistle.......................................surliness
Thistle, Scotch.........................retaliation
Thistle Seed Head ....depart
Thorn ....solace in adversity
Thorn, Branch of ....rigor, severity
Thrift ....sympathy
Throatwort............................neglected beauty
Thyme....................................activity
Thyme.......................................courage
Thyme.......................................thriftiness
Tiger Flower ....for once may pride befriend
                                        thee, pride befriend me
Toothwort...............................concealment
Trailing Arbutus....................simplicity
Tree of Life ....old age
Trembling Grass....................resistance, opposition
Tremella ....opposition, resistance
Tremella Nostoc ....resolve the riddle
Trillium Pictum ....modest beauty
Trillium Spinosum ....be prudent
Truffle....................................surprise
Trumpet Flower ....fame
Trumpet Flower.......................separation
Tuberose................................sweet voice, a sweet voice
Tuberose ....voluptuousness
Tuberose ....dangerous pleasures
Tulip......................................beautiful eyes
Tulip ....charity
Tulip ....fame
Tulip, Red.................................declaration of love
Tulip Tree.................................fame

Tulip Tree ....rural happiness
Tulip, Yellow ....hopeless love
Turnip..................................charity

U
Unique Rose ....call me not beautiful
Ulex ....anger

V
Valerian ....accommodating or obliging
                                  disposition, readiness
Valerian, Greek ....rupture
Venus's Car............................fly with me
Venus's Flytrap......................deceit
Venus's Flytrap......................have I caught you at last?
Venus's Looking Glass...........flattery
Verbena ....sensibility
Verbena ....sensitiveness
Verbena, Pink ....family union
Verbena, Scarlet ....church unity, unite against evil
Verbena, White ....pray for me
Veronica ....fidelity
Veronica Speciosa....................keep this for my sake
Vervain ....enchantment
Vervain ....superstition
Vine...drunkenness, intoxication
Violet......................................faith, faithfulness
Violet.......................................modesty
Violet, Dame ....watchfulness
Violet, Small White ....innocence and candor
Violet, White ....candor
Violet, White ....innocence
Violet, White ....purity of sentiment
Violet, Yellow ....rural happiness
Virginia Creeper....................I cling to you both in sunshine and shade
Viscaria Oculata ....will you dance with me?
Volkameria...............................may you be happy

W

Wallflower..............................bonds of affection

Wallflower..............................faithfulness/fidelity in adversity/misfortune

Wallflower..............................lasting beauty

Wallflower..............................she is fair

Walnut..................................intellect

Walnut ....stratagem

Walnut ....understanding

Watcher by the Wayside ....never despair

Water Lily..............................eloquence

Water Lily ....estranged love

Water Lily ....purity of heart

Water Lily ....repose

Water Lily ....silence

Water Lily Leaf........................recantation

Water Star................................beauty combined with piety

Watermelon............................bulkiness

Wax Plant..............................susceptibility

Wheat....................................prosperity, riches

Whortleberry ....treachery, treason

Willow....................................forsaken

Willow, Creeping ....love forsaken

Willow, French.........................bravery and humanity

Willow, Herb............................celibacy

Willow, Herb............................pretension

Willow, Weeping ....forsaken, forsaken lover

Willow, Weeping ....mourning

Willow, Weeping ....melancholy

Winter Cherry ....deception

Wisteria ....welcome, fair stranger

Witch Hazel............................spell, a spell, witchery

Wormwood............................absence

X

Xanthium................................pertinacity, rudeness

Xeranthemum ....cheerfulness under adversity

100

Y

Yarrow......................................cure for the heartache

Yarrow......................................thou alone canst cure

Yarrow......................................war

Yew ....penitence

Yew ....sadness, sorrow

Yucca......................................authority

Z

Zephyr Flower ....expectation

Zephyr Flower..........................sickness

Zinnia......................................absence, I mourn your absence

Zinnia ....thoughts of absent friends

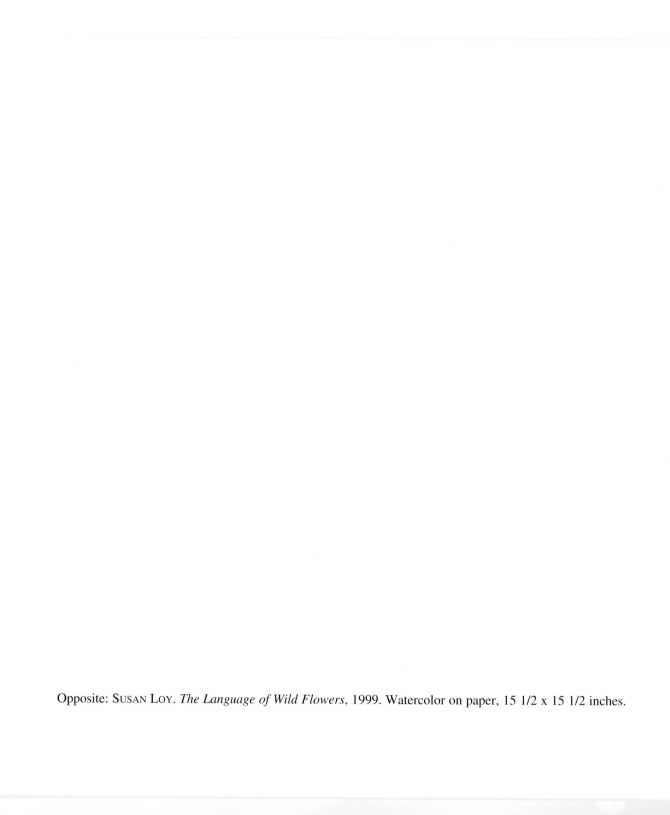

Opposite: SUSAN LOY. *The Language of Wild Flowers*, 1999. Watercolor on paper, 15 1/2 x 15 1/2 inches.

"The scenery, when it is truly seen, reacts on the life of the seer. How to live. How to get the most of life. How to extract its honey from the flower of the world." September 7, 1851, Journal of Henry David Thoreau

"Where the most beautiful wild-flowers grow; there one's spirit is fed and poets grow." June 1st, 1852, Journal of Henry David Thoreau

"Walking. ...Wildness is the preservation of the World.... Nature has a place for the wild clematis as well as for the cabbage."

DICTIONARY

OF

THE AMERICAN LANGUAGE OF FLOWERS

BY SENTIMENT

A

Abruptness, bluntness, rudeness..Borage
Absence...Wormwood, Zinnia
Abundance, plenty, riches ....Corn
Abuse not...Crocus
Acknowledgement...Bellflower, Lavender
Activity ....Thyme
Acute sorrow or affliction ....Aloe
Admiration..Amethyst
Adoration, your devout adorer ....Dwarf Sunflower
Adroitness, skill...Spider Orchis
Adulation ....Cacalia
Advice...Rhubarb
Affection..Amaranth, Morning Glory
                Moss, Pear, Sorrel

Affection, *see also* devoted/sacred affections
Affection beyond the grave ....Locust
Affection returned...Jonquil
Affliction...Black Poplar
Affliction, acute, *see* acute sorrow
Afterthought...Aster
Age..Snowball
Age, *see also* cheerfulness in old age, old age
Agitation ....Moving Plant
Agitation ....Sainfoin
Agreement..Corn Straw
Agriculture...Lucern
Aid, *see* help
Alas! for my poor heart ....Deep Red Carnation
Allurement, temptation...Quince
Always cheerful..Coreopsis
Always delightful ....Cineraria
Always lovely, you will always be lovely ....Double Indian Pink
Always remembered, never-ceasing remembrance...................Everlasting
Ambassador of love..Cabbage Rose
Ambition..Hollyhock, Mountain
                Laurel

Amiableness, amiability ....Jasmine
Amusement, frivolity, frivolous amusement ....Bladdernut
An old beau...Ice Plant
Anger ....Broom, Peony
Animosity ....Saint John's Wort
Anticipation ....Gooseberry
Anticipation, expectation...Anemone
Anxious, trembling ....Red Columbine
Appointed meeting ....Pea
Architecture ....Candytuft
Ardent attachment...Larkspur
Ardent love ....Cactus
Ardor...Broom
Ardor, zeal ....Arum
Argument ....Fig
Arrogance ....Lobelia
Art..Bear's-breech
Art, artifice, the arts, the fine arts...Acanthus
Artifice ....Catchfly
Artifice ....Clematis, Love-in-a-Mist
Aspiring ....Pyramidal Bellflower
Aspiring, you are aspiring ....Mountain Pink
Assiduity...Lavender
Assiduous to please ....Sprig of Ivy with Tendrils
Assignation, *see* rendezvous
Asylum, protection, succor...Juniper, Juniper Berries
Attachment, I attach myself to you ....Ipomoea
Audacity..Larch
Austerity ....Fuller's Teasel, Thistle
Authority..Yucca
Avarice...Scarlet Auricula
Aversion...China Pink, Indian Pink

B

Banquet, entertainment, feast, feasting, festivity ....Parsley
Bantering, jest, jesting ....Southernwood
Baseness, meanness ....Dodder

Bashful love..Damask Rose
Bashful modesty, bashfulness, modesty....................................Sensitive Plant
Bashful shame...Deep Red Rose
Bashfulness, bashful shame, shame ....Peony
Be mine...Four-leaved Clover
Be prudent..Trillium Spinosum
Be warned in time...Echites Atropurpurea
Beautiful eyes ....Tulip
Beautiful, but timid..Amaryllis
Beauty ....Parti-colored Daisy, Rose
Beauty, *see also* blushing, delicate, divine, feminine, fleeting,
    glorious, heartless, lasting, magnificent, mental, neglected,
    pensive, rustic, spiritual, transient, unconscious, and
    woodland beauty; *see also* innocence and beauty, pride
    and beauty, prosperity and beauty, purity and beauty,
    simplicity and beauty, worth above/beyond beauty
Beauty always/ever new ....China Rose
Beauty in retirement ....Aster, Rhodora
Beauty is vain ....Hibiscus
Beauty is your only attraction ....Japan Rose
Belle, a belle ....Orchis
Beloved daughter..Potentilla
Beneficence...Feverfew, Marsh Mallow,
                                                           Potato
Benefits..Spikenard
Benevolence...Calycanthus, Potato
Betrayal..Judas Tree, Catchfly
Beware ....Oleander, Rhododendron
Beware of false friends...Franciscea Latifolia
Beware of the coquette ....Catalpa Tree
Birth ....Dittany of Crete
Bitterness ....Aloe
Blackness ....Ebony Tree
Blessedness, *see* single blessedness
Bluntness, *see* abruptness
Blushes...Marjoram
Blushing beauty ....Damask Rose

Boaster ....Hydrangea
Boldness..Larch, Pink
Bonds ....Convolvulus
Bonds of affection ....Wallflower
Bonds of love..Honeysuckle
Bound..Snowball
Bound by fate ....Marsh Andromeda
Bounty...Double China Aster
Bravery ....False Dragon Head,
                                        Oak Leaf
Bravery and humanity ....French Willow
Bridal favor...Ivy Geranium
Bridal festivities..Orange Flowers
Brilliancy ....Poinsettia
Brilliant complexion, freshness of complexion........................Damask Rose
Bulk, extent...Gourd
Bulkiness...Watermelon
Bury me amid nature's beauties..Persimmon
Busybody ....Quamoclit

C
Call me not beautiful ....Unique Rose
Calm, calmness, calm repose, repose ....Buckbean
Calumny..Hellebore, Madder
Can you bear poverty?..Browallia
Candor...White Violet,
Capricious beauty ....Lady's Slipper, Musk Rose
Captivation..Field Convolvulus
Celibacy ....Bachelor's Button,
                                        Herb Willow
Change ....Pimpernel
Changeable disposition...Rye Grass
Charity ....Grape, Tulip, Turnip
Charm of a blush, The ....Cosmelia Subra
Charming ....Musk Rose
Charms..Sweet Balm
Charms, *see also* variety of charms

109

Charms of home ....Musk Rose

Charms, many charms ....China Rose, Multiflora
Rose

Chaste love, platonic love ....Rose Acacia

Chastity ....Orange, Orange Flowers,
Sensitive Plant

Cheerfulness ....Crocus

Cheerfulness, *see also* always cheerful

Cheerfulness in adversity ....Gorse

Cheerfulness in old age ....Aster

Cheerfulness under adversity ....Chinese Chrysanthemum

Childbirth...Dittany, Primrose,
Sweet William

Childhood, *see* memories of childhood

Childishness...Buttercup

Chivalry ....Daffodil

Chivalry, knight errantry ....Monkshood

Cleanliness...Hyssop

Cold-hearted, cold-heartedness, coldness................................Lettuce

Coldness, indifference ....Agnus Castus

Color of my fate, The ....Coral Honeysuckle

Come down, come down to me..Jacob's Ladder

Come, play...Hyacinth

Comfort..Pear Tree

Comforting, *see* consolation

Compassion..Allspice, Calycanthus,
Elder

Compensation or an equivalent ....Poor Robin

Complaint ....Ground Pine

Complaisance...Reed

Compliments, *see* my compliments

Concealed love, secret love..Acacia, Motherwort

Concealed merit, hidden merit, hidden worth.........................Coriander

Conceit...Nettle, Nettle Tree

Concord..Lote Tree

Confession ....Lavender

Confession, confession of love..Rosebud

Confidence ....Auricula, Geranium,
                                                                    Hepatica
Confidence in heaven ....Flowering Reed
Confiding love ....Globe-flowered Fuchsia
Conjugal love, conjugal fidelity ....Linden or Lime Tree
Conquer your love ....Milkweed
Consolation ....Snowdrop
Consolation, comforting ....Scarlet Geranium
Consolation, consolation of sleep or to the sick.......................Poppy
Constancy ....Bellflower, Box, Hyacinth
Constant heart, A ....Bellflower
Consumed by love ....Syrian Mallow
Contempt...Marigold, Yellow Sultan
Content, contentment, quiet happiness.....................................Houstonia
Contentment...Hoyabella
Coquetry ....Dandelion, Daphne,
                                                                    Day Lily, Yellow Lily
Cordiality, warmth of feeling or sentiment, warmth.................Peppermint
Counterfeit ....Mock Orange
Country life..Oats
Courage...Black Poplar, Thyme
Courtesy ....Manrandia
Craftiness ....Sweet William
Crime ....Tamarisk
Critic ....Squirting Cucumber
Cruelty ....Marigold, Nettle
Cure..Balm of Gilead
Cure for heartache ....Cranberry, Butterfly Weed,
                                                                    Yarrow
Curiosity ....Walking Fern, Sycamore

D
Dance, *see* will you dance with me?
Danger..Dragon's Claw,
                                                                    Rhododendron
Dangerous insinuation ....Convolvulus
Dangerous pleasures ....Tuberose

111

Dark thoughts ....Nightshade
Daughter, beloved, *see* beloved daughter
Deadly foe is near, A ....Monkshood
Death...Cypress, Nightshade
Death and eternal sorrow...Cypress Tree
Death preferable to loss of innocence ....Dried White Rose
Deceit...Adder's Tongue, Datura,
                                        Dogsbane, Geranium,
                                        Monkshood, Venus
                                        Flytrap
Deceit and ferocity ....Arum
Deceitful charms...Datura
Deceitful hope..Daffodil
Deception..White Cherry, Winter
                                        Cherry
Deceptive appearances ....Chestnut
Deceptive hopes...Celandine
Declaration of love ....Tulip
Decrease of love ....Yellow Sweetbriar Rose
Deeply interesting..Siberian Crab Tree
Defect, fault, imperfection..Henbane
Defense, protection...Privet
Deformity..Begonia
Dejection...Lichen
Dejection, sorrow..Lupine
Delay..Eupatorium
Delicacy ....Corn Flower
Delicate and lonely as this flower ....Bellflower
Delicate beauty ....Hibiscus
Delicate feelings ....Sensitive Plant
Delicate pleasure...Sweet Pea
Delicate simplicity..Lily of the Valley
Delirium..Foxglove
Delusive hope ....False Narcissus
Depart ....Dandelion, Thistle Seed
Departure ....Sweet Pea
Desertion...Columbine

112

Design ....Dyer's Weed

Desire ....Jonquil

Desire to please, I desire to please ....Daphne

Despair ....Almond, Cypress,
                                      Marigold and Cypress

Despair not; God is everywhere ....White Julienne

Despondency...Mourning Geranium,
                                      Humbleplant

Detraction ....Clotbur

Devoted love, generous and devoted affections........................Honeysuckle

Devotion ....Cross of Jerusalem

Devotion, devoted attachment ....Heliotrope

Dexterity ....Sweet William

Difficulty..Blackthorn

Diffidence ....Cyclamen, Red-leaved Rose

Dignity ....Clove, Dahlia, Elm,
                                      Laurel-leaved Magnolia,
                                      Rosebay

Dignity and elegance, *see* elegance and dignity

Dignity and meekness...Plumbago

Dignity of mind ....Hundred-leaved Rose

Disappointed hopes...Cypress

Disappointment..Syringa

Discretion...Lemon

Discussion..Pride of China

Disdain..Rue

Disdain, *see* contempt

Disguise ....Datura

Disgust ....Frog Ophrys

Dissension..Pride of China,
                                      Broken Straw

Distinction..Cardinal Flower

Distrust..Buttercup

Distrust, *see also* mistrust

Divine beauty...American Cowslip

Do me justice, render me justice ....Chestnut Tree

Do not abuse ....Saffron Flower

Do not refuse me ....Eschscholtzia
Docility ....Bulrush
Does he possess riches? ....Golden Bartonia
Domestic happiness ....Holly
Domestic industry ....Flax, Houseleek
Domestic virtue ....Sage
Doubt ....Apricot Blossom
Dreams, reverie ....Flowering Fern, Osmunda
Drunkenness, intoxication ....Vine
Dullness, indolence ....Mitraria Coccinea
Durability, duration ....Dogwood

E
Early attachment ....Thornless Rose
Early friendship, early and sincere friendship ....Periwinkle
Early youth ....Primrose
Ecstasy ....Lophospermum
Education, good education ....Cherry, Cherry Tree
Egotism ....Narcissus
Elegance ....Acacia, Locust Tree,
                                                                                                       Rose Acacia

Elegance, *see also* grace
Elegance and dignity ....Dahlia
Elegance, gracefulness ....Birch
Elevation ....Pine
Eloquence ....Crape Myrtle, Water Lily
Embarrassment ....Love in a Puzzle
Emulation ....Asparagus
Enchantment ....Vervain
Encouragement ....Golden Rod
Energy ....Salvia
Energy in adversity ....Chamomile
Enjoyment ....Ground Ivy
Ennui ....Moss
Entertainment, *see* banquet
Enthusiasm ....Gum Tree
Envy ....Bramble, Crowsbill

Equivalent, *see* compensation
Error ....Bee Ophrys, Orchis
Esteem...Sage
Esteem, not love ....Spiderwort,
               Strawberry Tree
Estimation..Indian Mallow
Estranged love ....Water Lily
Estrangement ....Citron
Eternity ....Eternal Flower
Evanescent pleasure...Red Poppy
Ever till now ....Lychnis
Excellence, *see* unpretending excellence
Excess is dangerous, beware of excess ....Saffron Flower
Excessive sensibility..Aspen, Aspen Tree
Exhilaration..Snowdrop Tree
Expectation, *see* anticipation
Expected meeting ....Nutmeg Geranium
Experience ....Sarsaparilla
Extent, *see* bulk
Extinguished hopes...Convolvulus Major
Eyes, *see* beautiful eyes

F
Facility ....Speedwell, Pyrus
               Japonica
Faith...Pine, Passion Flower
Faith, faithfulness ....Violet
Faithfulness...Heliotrope
Faithfulness in adversity, fidelity in adversity or misfortune ....Wallflower
Falsehood, *see* deceit
False riches ....Sunflower, Bugloss,
               Yellow Lily, Nightshade,
               Manchineel Tree
Fame ....Trumpet Flower, Tulip,
               Tulip Tree
Fame speaks you/him great and good ....Apple Blossom
Family union..Verbena, Pink

115

Fantastic extravagance ....Poppy
Farewell ....Aster, Pine, Spruce
Fascination ....Enchanter's Nightshade,
                                             Fern, Honesty
Fashion, fashionable, she will be fashionable ....Rocket
Fastidiousness ....Field Lilac, Purple Lilac
Fate ....Flax, Hemp
Fault, *see* defect
Favor ....Sassafras
Fear ....Arethusa, Aspen Tree
Feast, feasting, *see* banquet
Fecundity, *see* fruitfulness
Felicity, happiness ....Sweet Sultan
Female fidelity ....Speedwell
Female loveliness, the perfection of female loveliness ....Justicia
Feminine beauty ....Calla Lily
Feminine modesty ....Calla
Festivity, *see* banquet
Fickleness ....Abatina, Lady's Slipper
Fickleness, inconstancy ....Larkspur
Fidelity ....Honeysuckle, Ivy, Plum,
                                             Rosemary, Speedwell
Fidelity in love ....Lemon Blossom
Fidelity, *see* conjugal fidelity, female fidelity
Filial affection, filial love ....Clematis
Fine arts, *see* art
Finesse ....Sweet William
Fire ....Fraxinella
Fire, I burn ....Iris
First emotions of love, awakening love ....Lilac
Fitness ....Sweet Flag
Flame, flame of love ....Yellow Iris
Flattery ....Venus's Looking Glass
Flattery's smile ....Buckbean
Flee away ....Pennyroyal
Fleeting beauty ....Withered Rose
Fly with me ....Venus's Car

Follow me ....Star of Bethlehem
Folly ....Columbine
Folly, stupidity ....Scarlet Geranium
Foolishness, foppishness, fatuity ....Pomegranate
Foppery ....Cockscomb
Foresight ....Holly, Strawberry Blossom
Forever thine...Dahlia
Forget me not..Forget Me Not
Forgetfulness..Honesty, Poppy
Forgiveness...Lemon Verbena
Forlornness ....Wood Anemone
Formality...Ice Plant
Forsaken...Anemone, Laburnum,
                                                                              Lilac, Dark China Rose
Forsaken...Willow
Forsaken, forsaken lover ....Weeping Willow
Fortitude...Dipteracanthus Spectablis,
                                                                              English Moss
Fragrance ....Camphire
Frailty...Anemone
Frankness ....Osier
Fraternal love..Honeysuckle
Fraternal affection, love or sympathy ....Syringa
Friend in need, friendship in adversity.................Snowdrop
Friendship ....Joy, Rose Acacia
Friendship, *see also* early, true or unchanging friendship
Friendship, lasting friendship ....Ivy
Frivolity ....London Pride
Frivolity, frivolous amusement, *see* amusement
Frozen kindness ....Hoarhound
Frugality...Endive
Frugality, prudent economy.................................Chicory
Fruitfulness, fecundity ....Hollyhock
Future happiness...Celandine

117

G

Gaiety..Butterfly Ophrys, Butterfly Orchis

Gaiety, playful gaiety ....Yellow Lily

Gain, profit..Cabbage, Nosegay

Gallantry ....Sweet William

Game..Hyacinth

Generosity..Orange Tree

Genius..Plane Tree

Genteel, gentility ....Corn Cockle, Geranium, Pompon Rose

Gift, a gift ....Entoca

Girlhood...White Rosebud

Gladness...Myrrh

Gladness, *see also* youthful gladness

Glorious beauty..Glory Flower

Glory ....Beech, Daphne, Hickory, Laurel

Good nature ....Mullein

Good wishes ....Basil

Goodness..Goosefoot, Mallow, Mercury

Goodness, *see also* perfect excellence

Gossip ....Cobaea

Grace..China Rose, Fuchsia, Multiflora Rose, Rue

Grace, *see also* native grace

Grace and elegance...Yellow Jasmine

Grace, the graces ....Hundred-leaved Rose

Gracefulness, *see* elegance

Grandeur ....Ash, Ash Tree, Beech

Gratitude ....Agrimony, Bellflower

Greatness..Cotton Plant

Grief..Aloe, Bellflower, Hyacinth, Marigold

Growing old, I do not fear to grow old ....Autumn Crocus

Guidance..Star of Bethlehem

H

Happiness...Mudwort, Mugwort
Happiness, *see also* content, felicity, future happiness,
   momentary/transient happiness,
   return of happiness, rural happiness
Happy at all times...Coreopsis
Happy love...Bridal Rose
Hardihood, hardiness..Cranberry
Hate, hatred...Basil
Haughtiness..Larkspur, Tall Sunflower
Haughtiness, pride ....Amaryllis
Have confidence in me ....Primrose
Have I caught you at last? ....Venus's Flytrap
Healing...Balm of Gilead
Health...Balsam, Ice Moss,
                                    Iceland Moss

Heart, *see* constant heart, A
Heart left to desolation, A ....Yellow Chrysanthemum
Heart unacquainted with love................................White Rosebud
Heart withering in secret, The ....Lily of the Valley
Heart's mystery, The..Crimson Polyanthus
Heartless beauty...Dahlia
Heartlessness..Hydrangea
Heedlessness, thoughtlessness................................Almond, Almond Tree
Help, aid...Juniper, Juniper Berries
Hermitage ....Milkwort
Heroism..Nasturtium
Hidden qualities ....Sweet Potato
Hidden worth, *see* concealed merit
High-bred..Penstemon
High-souled..Scarlet Lily,
                                    Laurel-leaved Magnolia
Holy love ....Passion Flower
Holy wishes ....Plumbago Larpenta
Home..Rose
Honesty ....Dogwood, Honesty
Honor ....Oak

Honor, *see* uprightness

Hope ....Flowering Almond,
Bird Cherry,
Hawthorn, Snowdrop

Hope and innocence, *see* innocence and hope

Hope for better days ....Marianthus

Hope in adversity...Pine, Spruce

Hope in love ....Lychnis

Hope in misery ....Globe Amaranth

Hopeless, *see* withered hopes

Hopeless love...Yellow Tulip

Hopeless, not heartless ....Love-Lies-Bleeding

Horror ....Serpentine Cactus,
Cereus, Dragonwort,
Mandrake, Snakesfoot

Hospitality..Oak, Oak Tree

How came you here? ....Walking Leaf

Humanity ....Marsh Mallow, Oak Leaf

Humanity and bravery, *see* bravery and humanity

Humble love ....Fuchsia

Humility..Broom, Convolvulus
Field Lilac

Hypocrisy...Bugloss, Ebony

I

I am cured...Balm of Gilead

I am in despair ....Withered White Rose

I am more faithful than thou....................................Evening Primrose

I am not a summer friend ....Snowdrop

I am not ambitious for myself, but for you ....Foxglove

I am not changed ....Foxglove

I am sensible of your kindness, I feel your kindness.................Flax

I am worthy of you...White Rose

I am your captive...Peach Blossom

I am too happy...Cape Jasmine

I attach myself to you..Indian Jasmine

I burn...Common Cactus

I can't entirely trust you	Mushroom
I cannot give thee up	Columbine
I change but in dying	Laurel
I change not, unchangeable	Globe Amaranth
I claim, at least, your esteem	Potentilla
I cling to you both in sunshine and shade	Virginia Creeper
I declare against you	Belvedere, Wild Licorice
I declare war against you	Wild Tansy
I desire a return of affection	Jonquil
I die if neglected, I die if I'm neglected	Laurestina, Laurustinus
I dreamed of thee	Datura
I feel my obligations	Lint
I forgive you	Sultan, Lilac
I have dreamed of thee	Honeysuckle, Trumpet
I have found one true heart	Ivy
I have lost all	Mourning Bride
I live for thee	Cedar Leaf
I love	Red Chrysanthemum
I love you best when you are sad	Gentian
I mourn your absence	Zinnia
I offer you my all	Shepherd's Purse
I offer you pecuniary assistance, I offer you my fortune	Calceolaria
I partake your sentiments	Double China Aster
I partake, reciprocate, share your affections or sentiments	Garden Daisy
I promise	Clover
I reject you	Black Hoarhound
I respect thy tears	Bayberry
I rise above all, I surmount all difficulties or obstacles	Mistletoe
I shall die tomorrow	Gum Cistus
I shall not survive you	Black Mulberry Tree
I think of thee	Cedar
I trust thee, I turn to thee	Heliotrope
I value your sympathy	Monarda
I will enlighten you	Bayberry
I will not trouble you	Rose Leaf
I will think of it	Single China Aster, White Daisy, Wild Daisies

I with the morning's love have made sport ....Bachelor's Button
I wound to heal ....Eglantine, Rose
Idleness ....Mesembryanthemum
If you love me, you will find it out ....Maiden-blush Rose
Ill nature, ill temper, petulance, sour disposition ....Barberry, Crab Blossom
Ill-natured beauty..Citron
Imagination ....Aloe, American
               Eglantine, Lupine
Immortality ....Amaranth, American
               Arbor Vitae, Daphne,
               Globe Amaranth
Impatience..Balsam, Balsamine,
               Cuphea
Impatience/impatient of absence ....Corchorus
Impatient resolve ....Red Balsam
Imperfection, *see* defect
Imperial power...Crown Imperial
Importunity ....Burdock, Convolvulus,
               Thistle
Incense of a faithful heart, The ....Frankincense
Inconstancy...Evening Primrose, Wild
               Honeysuckle
Inconstancy, *see also* fickleness
Incorruptible ....Cedar of Lebanon
Indecision..Bulrush
Independence ....White Oak, Wild Plum
               Tree, Thistle
Indifference, *see also* coldness...Candytuft, Mustard,
               Pigeon Berry, Senvy
Indiscretion ....Common Almond,
               Bulrush, Reed
Indolence, *see* dullness
Industry ....Bee Orchis, Clover
Infatuation...Cardamine
Infatuation, I love you ....Heliotrope
Infidelity, unfaithfulness...Yellow Rose
Ingeniousness..White Pink

Ingenuity ....Penciled-leaf Geranium
Ingenuous simplicity...Mouse-eared Chickweed
Ingratitude ....Buttercup, Yellow Gen-
                                          tian, Thornless Rose
Injustice..Hops
Innocence ....Daisy, Dwarf Pink,
                                          White Violet
Innocence and beauty, beauty and innocence ....Daisy
Innocence and candor...Small White Violet
Innocence and hope ....Daisy
Inquietude ....Marigold
Insincerity ....Foxglove
Insinuation ....Convolvulus
Inspiration ....Angelica
Instability ....Dahlia
Instinct ....Pitcher Plant
Instruction ....Bayberry
Intellect ....Walnut
Intellectual excellence ....Venice Sumac
Intoxication ....Groundsel Tree
Intoxication, *see also* drunkenness
Intoxication, intoxicated with pleasure ....Heliotrope
Intrinsic worth..Gentian
Intrusion ....Bouncing Bess
Irony..Sardonia, Sardony

J
Jealousy...Hyacinth, French
                                          Marigold, Yellow Rose
Joking..Gentle Balm
Joy...Wood Sorrel
Joy, *see also* transport of joy
Joy of worth...White Lilac
Joys to come ....Celandine
Juice ....Rudbeckia
Justice to you, you shall have justice ....Coltsfoot

K

Keep this for my sake...Veronica Speciosa
Keep your promises...Petunia, Plum Tree
Kindness ....Pompon Rose
Knight errantry, *see* chivalry

L

Labor...Sorghum
Lady, deign to smile ....Oak Geranium
Lamentation ....Aspen Tree
Lasting beauty..Wallflower
Lasting love ....Chinese Primrose
Lasting pleasure...Everlasting Pea, Pea
Let me go...Butterfly Weed
Let me heal thy grief ....Arnica
Let us follow Jesus ....Star of Bethlehem
Let us forget...Yellow Rose
Levity, lightness...Daily Rose, Larkspur
Liberty...Live Oak
Life...Lucern
Lightheartedness..White Clover
Light of our path, The ....Star of Bethlehem
Lightning...Pomegranate
Live for me ....Arbor Vitae
Lively and pure affection, pure and ardent love ....Pink
Lofty aspirations or thoughts, lofty and pure thoughts ....Ailantus, Sunflower
Longevity..Fig
Love ....Myrtle, Rose
Love, *see also* ambassador of, chaste, concealed, confession
  of, confiding, conjugal, conquer your, consumed by,
  declaration of, decrease of, devoted, estranged,
  fidelity in, first emotions of, flame of, fraternal,
  happy, hopeless, humble, lasting, only deserve my,
  passionate, pretended, pure, too young to, transient,
  true, unrequited, wedded, woman's, and youthful love;
  see also esteem, I love, I love you best when you are sad,
  lively and pure affection, lovely and pure affection

Love at first sight..Coreopsis
Love, constant, but hopeless...Cinquefoil
Love forsaken ....Creeping Willow
Love in absence ....Myrtle
Love in a snow mist ....Daphne
Love in idleness...Pansy
Love is dangerous...Carolina Rose
Love of nature...Magnolia
Love of variety, variety, variety is charming ....China Aster
Love, pleasure and pain..Dog Rose
Love returned..Ambrosia
Love sweet and secret, my love is sweet and secret ....Honey Flower
Love undiminished by adversity ....Dogwood
Loveliness, *see* female, perfect, and supreme loveliness
Loveliness and cheerfulness..Chinese Chrysanthemum
Loveliness, pretty, prettiness ....Pompon Rose
Loveliness, thou art all that is lovely ....Austrian Rose
Lovely, *see* always lovely, pure and lovely
Lovely and pure affection..White Pink
Lovers' tryst ....Beech
Love's memory, love and memory ....Laurel
Love's messenger...Rose Campion
Love's oracle..Dandelion
Lowliness...Bramble
Luster ....Aconite-leaved Crowfoot
Luxury...Chestnut, Chestnut Tree
Luxury, luxuriancy ....Horse Chestnut

M
Magic ....Angelica, Fern
Magnificent beauty ....Calla
Magnificence ....Magnolia
Majesty ....Crown Imperial, Lily
Make haste...Dianthus
Malevolence...Lobelia
Manners, morals ....Wild Rue
Marriage..Citron, Saffron

125

Marriage, matrimony, *see also* wedded love
Maternal affection...Cinquefoil
Maternal care ....Coltsfoot
Maternal love ....Moss
Maternal tenderness...Sorrel, Wood
Matrimony ....American Linden
Matronly grace..Pinelia Cattleya
Mature charms ....Cattleya
Mature elegance..Pomegranate Flower
May you be happy ....Volkalmeria
Meanness, *see* baseness
Medicine ....Butterfly Weed, Endive
Meekness ....Birch
Meeting, a meeting ....Musk Plant
Meeting, *see also* appointed, expected, unexpected meeting
Melancholy ....Autumnal Leaves, Dark
                                                                                    Geranium, Dead Leaves,
                                                                                    Weeping Willow
Melancholy mind or spirit..Sorrowful Geranium
Memories of childhood...Buttercup
Memories, sad, *see* painful recollections
Memory, *see* pleasant or tender recollections ....Syringa
Mental beauty ....Kennedia, Kennedya
Mental beauty or mental excellence.....................................Clematis
Mercy...Chamomile
Merit ....Coriander
Merit, *see also* concealed, modest, superior, and
     unpatronized merit
Merit before beauty ....Sweet Alyssum
Message, I have a message for thee ....Iris
Mildness, mild or sweet disposition.....................................Mallow
Mirth ....Crocus, Wild Grape,
                                                                                    Pimpernel
Misanthropy..Monkshood, Thistle
Mistrust, distrust ....Lavender
Modest beauty...Trillium Pictum
Modest genius..Creeping Cereus

126

Modest merit..Camellia Japonica
Modest worth..Primrose
Modesty ....Calla, Violet
Modesty, *see also* bashful modesty
Momentary/transient happiness.................................Spiderwort
Moral and intellectual beauty....................................Mignonette
Mourning ....Cypress, Weeping Willow
Music ....Reed
Music, the witching soul of music ....Oats
My bane, my antidote..White Poppy
My best/happiest days are gone ....Meadow Saffron
My compliments...Iris
My destiny is in your hands ....Camellia
My regrets follow you to the grave............................Asphodel

N
Native grace...Cowslip
Neatness...Dyer's Broom
Necessity..Mermaid Weed
Neglected beauty ....Throatwort
Never despair...Watcher by the Wayside
Never forget...Thistle
Never-ceasing/unceasing remembrance ....Cudweed
Night ....Convolvulus, Ebenaster
No ....Snapdragon
Nobility..Queen of the Prairie
Nobility, *see also* true nobility
Novelty ....Calceolaria

O
Oblivion ....Poppy
Obstacle ....Ox Eye
Obstacles to be overcome/surmounted.......................Mistletoe
Obstinacy ....Convolvulus
Offense...Stapelia
Old age...Tree of Life
Omen, presage ....Small Cape Marigold

Only deserve my love..Rose Campion
Opinion ....Escallonia
Opportunity..Phaseolus
Opposition, resistance...Tremella
Oracle, rustic oracle, love's oracle...Dandelion
Ornament ....Hornbeam
Ostentation...Peony
Our souls are united..Phlox

P
Painful recollections, sad memories...Adonis
Painting ....Auricula
Painting the lily..Daphne Odora
Parasite..Mistletoe
Parental affection, parental love ....Cinquefoil, Wild Sorrel
Participation...Double Daisy
Passion...White Dittany of Crete
Passion, flame of love ....Yellow Iris
Passionate love ....Passion Flower
Paternal error ....Cardamine
Patience...Crocus, Dock, Ox Eye,
                                                                                  Rest Harrow
Patriotism...American Elm, Nasturtium
Peace ....Hazel, Olive
Peerless and proud..Magnolia
Penitence..Yew
Pensive beauty ....Laburnum
Pensiveness..Cowslip
Perfect excellence/goodness, perfection....................................Strawberry
Perfect loveliness..Camellia
Perfection, you are perfect...Pineapple
Perfidity ....Laurel in Flower
Perplexity, *see* you puzzle me
Persecution...Fritillaria
Perseverance ....Canary Grass, Ground
                                                                                   Laurel, Swamp Marigold,
                                                                                   Strawberry Tree

Persuasion ....Syrian Mallow
Pertinacity ....Xanthium
Petulance, *see* ill temper
Philanthropy...Melilot
Philosophy ....Pine
Piety, *see* steadfast piety
Pity..Pine
Play ....Hyacinth
Pleasant or tender recollections, sweet remembrances ....Periwinkle
Pleasantry..Balm, Gentle Balm
Pleasure...Loasa
Pleasure, *see also* lasting pleasure
Pleasure and pain...Dog Rose
Pleasure without alloy ....Moss Rose
Plenty, *see* abundance
Poetry ....American Eglantine,
                                                                                            Eglantine
Politeness ....Ageratum
Pomp...Dahlia
Poor but happy, we may be poor, but we will be happy............Vernal Grass
Popular favor ....Cistus
Poverty ....Evergreen, Evergreen
                                                                                            Clematis
Poverty and worth...Evergreen
Power ....Cress, Crown Imperial
Praise..Meadowsweet
Pray for me. ....White Verbena
Precaution ....Golden Rod
Precocity ....May Rose
Prediction..Prophetic Marigold
Preference ....Apple Blossom,
                                                                                            Rose-scented Geranium,
                                                                                            Scarlet Geranium
Preferment...Cardinal Flower
Presumption ....Snapdragon
Pretended love ....Catchfly
Pretension ....Glasswort, Herb Willow

129

Pride ....Scarlet Auricula, Pink,
Hundred-leaved Rose

Pride, *see also* haughtiness, virgin pride

Pride and beauty ....Carnation, Pink

Pride befriend me, for once may pride befriend thee................Tiger Flower

Pride of birth..Crown Imperial

Pride of riches..Crown Imperial

Pride of riches, pride of newly acquired fortune.......................Auricula

Privation..Myrobalan

Prodigality..Dutchman's Pipe

Prohibition ....Privet

Prolific, profuseness ....Fig Tree

Promise ....White Clover

Promise, *see also* keep your promises

Promptness, promptitude ....Ten-Week Stock

Prosperity..Beech, Bryony,
Nemophila, Wheat

Prosperity and beauty ....Red-leaved Rose

Protection..Bearded Crepis, Cedar

Protection, *see also* asylum

Providence, provident..Clover, Oleaster

Proximity undesirable..Burdock

Prudence ....Mountain Ash,
Service Tree

Prudent economy, *see* frugality

Pure and lovely, may you ever be pure and lovely...................Red Rosebud

Pure love ....Pink

Purification ....Hyssop, Rue

Purity...Lily, Star of Bethlehem

Purity and beauty, modesty, or sweetness...............................Lily

Purity of heart ....Water Lily

Purity of sentiment ....White Violet

Purity, modesty...White Lilac

Q

Quarrel ....Broken Corn

Quick-sightedness..Hawkweed

R

Rarity ....Mandrake
Ready armed ....Gladiolus
Reason...Goat's Rue
Recall ....Silver-leaved Geranium
Recantation ....Water Lily Leaf
Reciprocity..Star Flower
Recollections, *see* painful, pleasant or tender,
   youthful recollections
Reconciliation ....Hazel, Star of Bethlehem
Refinement..Gardenia
Refusal ....Striped Carnation
Regard...Daffodil
Relief...Balm of Gilead
Relieve my anxiety. ....Christmas Rose
Religious enthusiasm..Schinus
Religious enthusiasm, a religious enthusiast...............Lychnis
Religious fervor ....Passion Flower
Religious superstition ....Aloe, Passion Flower
Remembered beyond the tomb.......................................Asphodel
Remembrance ....Adonis, Rosemary
Remembrance, *see also* pleasant recollections
Remembrance, never-ceasing; *see* always remembered
Remorse ....Bramble, Raspberry
Rendezvous..Chickweed
Rendezvous, assignation..Pimpernel
Repentance...Rue
Repose..Morning Glory,
                                                                                                 Water Lily
Repose, *see also* calm
Reproof ....Euphorbia
Rescue..Rock Maple
Resemblance, semblance ....Spiked Speedwell
Reserve ....Maple, Sycamore
Resignation ....Indian Cress
Resistance ....Tansy, Trembling Grass,
                                                                                                 Tremella

Resistance, *see also* opposition
Resolve the riddle ....Tremella Nostoc
Resolved to win ....Purple Columbine
Restoration...Persicaria
Retaliation...Scotch Thistle
Retirement..Lake Flower, Maple
Return of happiness ....Lily of the Valley
Revenge ....Clover
Reverie...Flowering Fern, Osmunda
Reverie, *see also* dreams
Reward of merit...Laurel
Reward of merit or virtue ....Crown of Roses
Riches, desire of riches, I wish I was rich, wealth....................Buttercup, Wheat
Riches, *see also* abundance, false riches, prosperity
Rigor ....Lantana, Branch of Thorns
Rivalry ....Rocket
Romance ....Azalea
Roughness of manner ....Borage
Royalty...Angrec
Rudeness...Clotbur
Rumor ....Mayweed
Rupture ....Greek Valerian
Rupture, rupture of a contract ....Broken Straw
Rural happiness..Tulip Tree
Rural happiness..Yellow Violet
Rustic beauty ....French Honeysuckle

S
Sacred affections..Yellow Marigold
Sadness ....Primrose, White Rose
Sadness, sorrow ....Leaf, Leaves, Yew
Safety ....Clematis
Satire ....Pepper Plant, Prickly Pear
Scandal...Hellebore
Skepticism..Nightshade
Sculpture ....Hoya

Secrecy...Full-blown Rose,
                                      Maidenhair Fern,
                                      White Rose
Self-love, self-esteem ....Narcissus
Self-sacrifice...Andromeda
Self-seeking ....Clianthus
Sensibility ....Verbena
Sensibility, sensitiveness ....Mimosa
Sensitiveness..Verbena
Sensuality..Spanish Jasmine
Separation ....Carolina Jasmine,
                                      Trumpet Flower
Serenade, a serenade...Dew Plant
Serenity, tranquility of mind ....Lemon Geranium
Severity ....Branch of Thorns
Shame, *see* bashful shame
Sharpness, tartness..Barberry
She is fair..Wallflower
Sick, *see* consolation to the sick
Sickness ....Anemone
Silence...White Rose, Water Lily
Silence, Hush!...Belladonna
Silent love ....Evening Primrose
Silliness...Fool's Parsley
Simplicity..American Eglantine, Dog
                                      Rose, Single Rose, Wild
                                      Rose, Trailing Arbutus
Simplicity, *see also* delicate simplicity
Simplicity and beauty ....Burgundy Rose
Sincerity..Garden Chervil, Fern
Single blessedness ....Corn Flower,
                                      Hackmetack
Singularity..Cockscomb,
Skill...Spider Orchis, Spider
                                      Ophrys
Skill, *see also* adroitness
Slander ....Nettle

133

Sleep, sleep of the heart, consolation of sleep .... Poppy
Slighted affections, slighted love .... Yellow Chrysanthemum
Smile on me still .... Sunflower
Smile, a smile .... Sweet William
Smile, *see also* lady, deign to smile
Smiles .... Crocus
Snare .... Dragon Plant
Snare, a snare .... Catchfly
Social intercourse .... Balm
Solace in adversity .... Everlasting Thorn
Solitude, solitude is sometimes the best society .... Heather, Lichen
Sorrow .... Cypress, Hyacinth
Sorrow, *see also* dejection, grief, sadness
Sorrowful, I am sorry .... Hyacinth
Sorrowful regret .... Bluebell
Soul of my soul .... Virginian Jessamine
Souls, *see* our souls are united
Sour disposition, sourness of temper, *see* ill nature
Spell .... Enchanter's Nightshade
Spell, a spell, witchery .... Witch Hazel
Spiritual strength .... Cedar
Spiritual beauty .... Cherry Blossom
Spleen .... Fumitory
Splendid beauty .... Amaryllis
Splendid misery .... Sumac
Splendor .... Auricula, Lobelia,
                                          Superb Lily, Sumac,
                                          Yellow Nasturtium
Sport .... Hyacinth
Sporting .... Foxtail Grass
Stability .... Cress
Star of my existence .... Chickweed
Stateliness .... Foxglove
Steadfast piety .... Wild Geranium
Stoicism .... Box
Stratagem .... Sweet William, Walnut
Strength .... Cedar, Fennel

Strength, *see also* spiritual strength
Strength of character...Gladiolus
Stupidity...Scarlet Geranium
Stupidity, *see also* folly
Submission...Bellflower, Grass
Success..Summer Savory
Success crown your wishes ....Coronella, Coronilla
Success everywhere ....Nemophila
Succor, *see* asylum
Such worth is rare...Achimenes Cupreata
Sun-beamed eyes ....Scarlet Lychnis
Superior merit...Moss Rose
Superstition..Saint John's Wort,
                                                                                      Vervain
Superstitious sanctity..Saint John's Wort
Supreme loveliness...Camellia Japonica
Surliness..Thistle
Surprise ....Betony, Truffle
Susceptibility ....Wax Plant
Suspense ....Ipomopsis
Suspicion...Mushroom
Sweet disposition...Mallow, Marsh
Sweet voice, a sweet voice......................................Tuberose
Sweetness..White Sultan
Sweetness, *see also* unconscious sweetness
Sweets of social intercourse ....Balm
Sweets to the sweet..Daphne
Swiftness..Larkspur
Sympathetic feeling ....Balm of Gilead
Sympathy ....Balm

T
Talent ....White Pink
Talisman ....Mountain Ash
Talking..Rhododendron
Tardiness...Flax-leaved Golden Locks
Taste...Scarlet Fuchsia

Tears ....Helenium
Temper, sharpness/sourness of temper, *see* ill temper
Temperance...Azalea
Temptation ....Apple, Apricot, Quince
Temptation, *see also* allurement
Tender and pleasant thoughts ....Pansy
Thankfulness...Agrimony
Thee only do I love..Arbutus
There is every thing to be gained by good company ....Rose in a Tuft of Grass
There is no unalloyed good ....Lapageria Rosea
Thine till death..American Arbor Vitae
Think of me ....Cedar, White Clover,
                              Pansy
This heart is thine ....Peach Blossom
Thou alone canst cure...Yarrow
Thou art changed ....Scarlet Geranium
Thou art less proud than they deem thee................................Petunia
Thoughtlessness, *see* heedlessness
Thoughts ....Pansy
Thoughts, *see also* tender and pleasant thoughts,
   you occupy my thoughts
Thoughts of absent friends ....Zinnia
Thoughts of heaven ....Snowball
Threats ....Rose-leaved Rubus
Thriftiness...Thyme
Thy frown will kill me ....Currant
Thy smile I aspire to...Daily Rose
Ties ....Tendrils
Time..Four-o'clock, Pine,
                              White Poplar
Timidity ....Amaryllis, Daphne,
                              Four-o'clock
To live without ....Agnus Castus
To win..Parsley
Token, a token ....Laurestina
Too young to love..White Rose, White
                              Rosebud

Touch me not..Burdock, Red Balsam
Tranquility, tranquility of mind..Lemon Geranium, Rock
                                          Madwort, Mudwort,
                                          Stonecrop

Tranquility, tranquility of mind, *see also* serenity
Tranquilize my anxiety..Christmas Rose
Transient beauty ....Night-blooming Cereus
Transient impressions ....Withered White Rose
Transient love ....Spiderwort
Transport of joy ....Cape Jasmine
Traveler's joy ....English Clematis
Treachery..Bilberry, Dahlia
Treachery, treason ....Whortleberry
Trifling beauty ....Hibiscus
Trifling character, a trifling character ....Bladdernut
True friendship ....Oak Geranium
True love..Forget Me Not
True nobility ....Dogwood
Truth ....White Chrysanthemum,
                                          Nightshade

U
Unanimity ....Phlox
Unbelief ....Judas Flowers, Judas Tree
Uncertainty ....Convolvulus, Daffodil
Unchanging friendship ....Arbor Vitae
Unconscious beauty..Burgundy Rose
Unconscious sweetness..Lily of the Valley
Understanding..Walnut
Uneasiness ....Garden Marigold
Unexpected meeting ....Geranium, Lemon
Unfortunate attachment ....Scabious
Union ....Whole Straw
Unite against evil, church unity..Scarlet Verbena
Unity ....White and Red Rose
Unpatronized merit..Primrose
Unpretending excellence ....Camellia Japonica

Unrequited love ....Daffodil
Uprightness, sentiments of honor ....Imbricaria
Usefulness, utility ....Grass
Uselessness ....Meadowsweet
Utility ....Dried Flax

V
Variety ....Portulaca, Rose Mundi
Variety, *see also* love of variety
Variety of charms ....China Aster
Variety of your conversation delights me, The ....Clarkia
Vice ....Darnel
Vicissitude ....Locust
Victory ....Palm
Virgin pride ....Gentian
Virtue ....Mint
Virtue is true beauty, virtue makes her charming ....Laurel
Vivacity ....Houseleek
Voice, *see* sweet voice
Volubility ....Abecedary
Voluptuousness ....Tuberose
Voraciousness ....Lupine
Vulgar minds, vulgar-minded ....African Marigold

W
War ....York and Lancaster Rose,
                                                                                             Yarrow
War-like trophy ....Indian Cress
Warmth of feeling or sentiment, *see* cordiality
Warmth of sentiment ....Spearmint
Warning ....Hand Flower Tree
Watchfulness ....Dame Violet
Weakness ....Musk Plant
Wealth is not happiness ....Scarlet Auricula
Wealth, *see* riches
Wedded love ....Beech
Wedded love, marriage, matrimony ....Ivy

138

Welcome to a stranger..Aster
Welcome, fair stranger ....Wisteria
White man's footsteps...Plantain
Widowhood...Sweet Scabious
Will you accompany me to the East?.......................................Stephanotis
Will you dance with me?...Viscaria Oculata
Will you help me? ....Andromeda
Will you pledge me?...Sidesaddle Flower
Will you share my fortunes? ....Malon Creeana
Wilt thou go? Wilt thou go away? Wilt thou go with me?..........Everlasting Pea
Win me and wear me...Lady's Slipper
Winning grace...Cowslip
Wisdom...Blue Salvia, Red Mul-
                                                                                                      berry, White Mulberry
Wit ....Lychnis, Meadow
Wit, wit ill-timed ....Sorrel
Witchery, *see* spell
With me you are safe...Mountain Ash
Withered hopes ....Anemone
Woman's love ....Red Pink
Woman's worth...Orange Blossom
Woodland beauty ....Sycamore
Worldliness ....Clianthus
Worth, *see* concealed merit, intrinsic worth, modest merit,
    modest worth, woman's worth, poverty and worth
Worth above beauty..Corn Cockle
Worth beyond beauty ....Sweet Alyssum
Worthy of praise, worthy all praise...Fennel

Y
You are aspiring, *see* aspiring
You are charming ....Leschenaultia Splendens
You are cold ....Hortensia, Hydrangea
You are dazzling, but dangerous ....Snapdragon
You are fair and fascinating ....White Pink, Variegated
                                                                                                      Pink
You are merry...Rose Mundi

You are my divinity...American Cowslip
You are radiant with charms ....Buttercup
You are rich in attractions ....Buttercup
You are spiteful ....Nettle
You are the queen of coquettes ....Queen's Rocket, Rocket
You are too bold ....Dipladenia Crassinoda
You are without pretension ....Rose Campion
You are without pretension, you have no claims ....Flora's Bells,
                                                                         Pasque Flower
You cannot deceive me ....Japanese Lilies
You excite my curiosity ....Molucca Balm
You have many lovers..Chorozema Varium
You may hope...Rose Leaf
You occupy my thoughts...Pansy
You please all ....Currants
You puzzle me, perplexity...Love-in-a-Mist
You terrify me ....Snake Cactus
You will always be lovely, *see* always lovely
You will be my death ....Hemlock
You worry me...Burr
Young girl, you are young and beautiful ....Rosebud
Your devout adorer, *see* adoration
Your eyes are bewitching..Eyebright
Your frown I defy...Anemone
Your charms are engraven on my heart ....Spindle Tree
Your looks freeze me, you freeze me.......................................Ice Plant
Your presence revives me ....Rosemary
Your presence softens my pain ....Milkvetch
Your presence soothes me...Petunia
Your purity equals your loveliness..Orange Blossom
Your qualities surpass your charms/loveliness ....Mignonette
Your qualities, like your charms, are unequalled.....................Peach
Your sentiments meet with a return ....China Aster
Your single elegance charms me..Diosma
Your temper is too hasty ....Grammanthes Chloraflora
Your whims are quite unbearable...Monarda Amplexicaulis

Youth ....Crocus, Damask Rose,
Foxglove, Primrose

Youth, *see also* early youth
Youth, youthful innocence ....White Lilac
Youthful beauty ....Cowslip
Youthful charms ....Rosebud
Youthful gladness ....Crocus
Youthful love ....Catchfly
Youthful recollections ....Dandelion

Z
Zeal, zealousness ....Elder
Zeal, zealousness, *see also* ardor
Zest ....Lemon

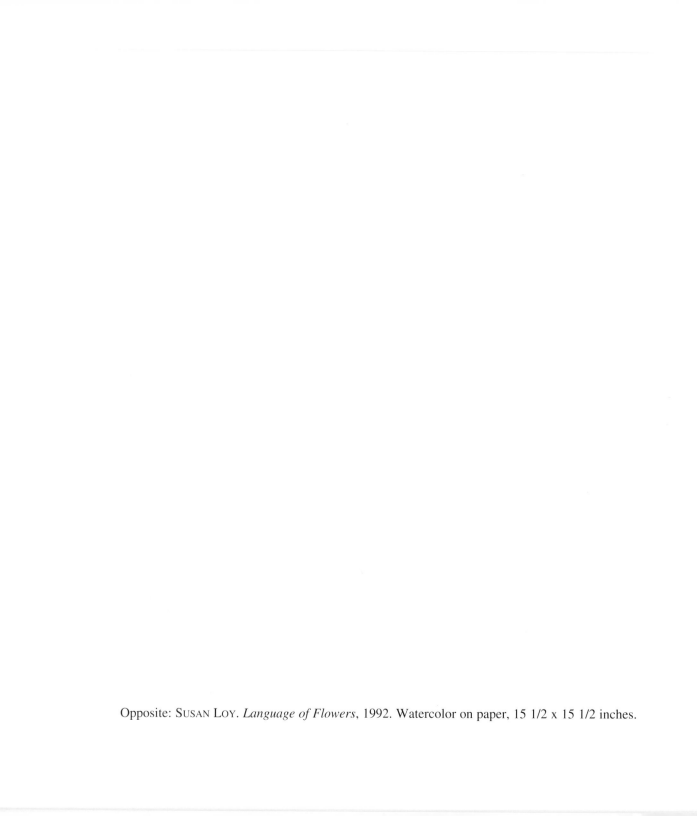

Opposite: Susan Loy. *Language of Flowers*, 1992. Watercolor on paper, 15 1/2 x 15 1/2 inches.

POETRY OF THE LANGUAGE OF FLOWERS

Flowers

Sarah Carter Edgarton Mayo

'T is said that in gorgeous Eastern climes,
Where folks are too idle for stringing rhymes,
When a lover would send to his lady a token
Of love, which in words may not be spoken,
He hies away to the garden bowers,
And culls a bouquet of the fairest flowers;
Which, woven together of magic art,
Are the language of love to the maiden's heart!

No tale of passion have I to breathe;
Yet, gentle reader, I fain would wreathe
A floral garland, whose leaves shall be
Emblems and tokens of love to thee.
FLOWERS!– they bloom by the lowliest cot–
May they gladden, and brighten, and bless thy lot!

Love Letters Made of Flowers

Leigh Hunt

An exquisite invention this,
Worthy of love's most honeyed kiss,
This art of writing *billet doux*
In buds and odors, and bright hues;
In saying all one feels and thinks
In clever daffodils and pinks,
Uttering (as well as silence may)
The sweetest words the sweetest way:
How fit, too, for the lady's bosom,
The place where *billet doux* repose 'em.

How charming in some rural spot,
Combining love with garden plot,
At once to cultivate one's flowers,
And one's epistolary powers,
Growing one's own choice words and fancies
In orange-tubs and beds of pansies;
One's sighs and passionate declarations
In odorous rhet'ric of carnations;
Seeing how far one's stocks will reach;
Taking due care one's flowers of speech
To guard from blight as well as bathos,
And watering every day one's pathos.

A letter comes just gathered; we
Dote on its tender brilliancy;
Inhale its delicate expression
Of balm and pea; and its confession
Made with as sweet a maiden blush
As ever morn bedewed in bush;
And then, when we have kissed its wit,
And heart, in water putting it,
To keep its remarks fresh, go round
Our little eloquent plot of ground,
And with delighted hands compose
Our answer, all of lily and rose,
Of tuberose and of violet,
And little darling (*mignonette*),
And gratitude and polyanthus,
And flowers that say, "Felt never man thus!"

146

The Language of Flowers
Charles F. Hoffman

Teach thee their language? sweet, I know no tongue,
    No mystic art those gentle things declare,
I ne'er could trace the schoolman's trick among
    Created things, so delicate and rare
Their language. Prythee! why they are themselves
    But bright thoughts syllabled to shape and hue,
The tongue that erst was spoken by the elves,
    When tenderness as yet within the world was new.

And still how oft their soft and starry eyes–
    Now bent to earth, to heaven now mutely pleading,
Their incense fainting as it seeks the skies,
    Yet still from earth with freshening hope receding–
How often these to every heart declare,
    With all the silent eloquence of truth,
The language that they speak is Nature's prayer,
    To give her back those spotless days of youth.

Flowers
Park Benjamin

Flowers are love's truest language; they betray,
    Like the divining rods of marigold,
    Where priceless wealth lies buried; not of gold,
But love, strong love, that never can decay!
I send thee flowers, O dearest! and I deem
    That from their petals then wilt hear sweet words,
    Whose music, clearer than the voice of birds,
When breathed to thee alone, perchance, may seem
All eloquent of feelings unexpressed.

The Language of Flowers

James Gates Percival

In Eastern lands they talk in Flowers,
  And they tell in a garland their Loves and Cares;
Each blossom that blooms in their garden bowers,
  On its leaves a mystic language bears.

The Rose is a sign of Joy and Love,
  Young, blushing Love in its earlier dawn;
And the mildness that suits the gentle dove,
  From the Myrtle's snowy flower is drawn.

Innocence shines in the Lily's bell,
  Pure as the heart in its native heaven
Fame's bright star and glory's swell,
  By the glossy leaf of the Bay are given.

The silent, soft, and humble heart
  In the Violet's hidden sweetness breathes;
And the tender soul that cannot part,
  A twine of Evergreen fondly wreathes.

The Cypress that daily shades the grave
  Is Sorrow that mourns her bitter lot,
And Faith that a thousand ills can brave
  Speaks in thy blue leaves – Forget-me-not.

Then gather a wreath from the garden bowers.
And tell the wish of thy heart in flowers.

A Flower in a Letter

Elizabeth Barrett Browning

Love's language may be talked with these;
To work out choicest sentences,
　　No blossoms can be meeter;
And, such being used in Eastern bowers,
Young maids may wonder if the flowers
　　Or meanings be the sweeter.

And such being strewn before a bride,
Her little foot may turn aside,
　　Their longer bloom decreeing,
Unless some voice's whispered sound
Should make her gaze upon the ground
　　Too earnestly for seeing.

And such being scattered on a grave,
Whoever mourneth there, may have
　　A type which seemeth worthy
Of that fair body hid below,
Which bloomed on earth a time ago,
　　Then perished as the earthy.

And such being wreathed for worldly feast,
Across the brimming cup some guest
　　Their rainbow colors viewing,
May feel them, with a silent start,
The covenant his childish heart
　　With Nature made, – renewing.

Flowers

Henry Wadsworth Longfellow

Spake full well, in language quaint and olden,
    One who dwelleth by the castled Rhine,
When he called the flowers, so blue and golden,
    Stars, that in earth's firmament do shine.

Stars they are, wherein we read our history,
    As astrologers and seers of eld;
Yet not wrapped about with awful mystery,
    Like the burning stars, which they beheld.

Wondrous truths, and manifold as wondrous,
    God hath written in those stars above;
But not less in the bright flowerets under us
    Stands the revelation of his love.

Bright and glorious is that revelation,
    Written all over this great world of ours;
Making evident our own creation,
    In these stars of earth, these golden flowers.

And the Poet, faithful and far-seeing,
    Sees, alike in stars and flowers, a part
Of the self-same, universal being,
    Which is throbbing in his brain and heart.

Gorgeous flowerets in the sunlight shining,
    Blossoms flaunting in the eye of day,
Tremulous leaves, with soft and silver lining,
    Buds that open only to decay;

Brilliant hopes, all woven in gorgeous tissues,
    Flaunting gayly in the golden light;
Large desires, with most uncertain issues,
    Tender wishes, blossoming at night!

These in flowers and men are more than seeming,
    Workings are they of the self-same powers,
Which the Poet, in no idle dreaming,
    Seeth in himself and in the flowers.

Everywhere about us are they glowing,
    Some like stars, to tell us Spring is born;
Others, their blue eyes with tears o'er flowing,
    Stand like Ruth amid the golden corn;

Not alone in Spring's armorial bearing,
    And in Summer's green-emblazoned field,
But in arms of brave old Autumn's wearing,
    In the centre of his brazen shield;

Not alone in meadows and green alleys,
    On the mountain-top, and by the brink
Of sequestered pools in woodland valleys,
    Where the slaves of nature stoop to drink;

Not alone in her vast dome of glory,
    Not on graves of bird and beast alone,
But in old cathedrals, high and hoary,
    On the tombs of heroes, carved in stone;

In the cottage of the rudest peasant,
    In ancestral homes, whose crumbling towers,
Speaking of the Past unto the Present,
    Tell us of the ancient Games of Flowers;

In all places, then, and in all seasons,
    Flowers expand their light and soul-like wings,
Teaching us, by most persuasive reasons,
    How akin they are to human things.

And with childlike, credulous affection,
    We behold their tender buds expand;
Emblems of our own great resurrection,
    Emblems of the bright and better land.

The Language of Flowers
Catharine H. Waterman Esling

Earth hath a thousand tongues, that swell
   In converse soft, and low–
We hear them in the flowery dell,
   And where the waters flow.
We note them when the pliant reed
   Bends to the summer air,
Its low-toned music gently freed
   By the soft breezes there;
And angels from their starry height,
On hills, and dales, and green banks write.

There is a language in each flower
   That opens to the eye,
A voiceless – but a magic power,
   Doth in earth's blossoms lie;
The flowering Almond, first to bring
   Its perfume to the breeze,
The earliest at the call of spring,
   Among the green-clad trees,
Whispers of Indiscretion's fate,
Trusting too soon – convinced too late....

Yes – flowers have tones – God gave to each
   A language of its own,
And bade the simple blossom teach
   Where'er its seed are sown;
His voice is on the mountain's height
   And by the river's side,
Where flowers blush in glowing light,
   In Lowliness, or Pride;
We feel, o'er all the blooming sod,
It is the language of our God.

152

APPENDIX

The appendix provides a translation of Latour's French dictionary of flower associations as well as twelve American language of flower dictionaries and three British. Each book has a one or two-letter code (**in bold**), which is used in the appendix. The code is based on the name of the author, editor, or publisher.

I have presented the flower nomenclature much as it appears in the original dictionaries, retaining many of the now dated or hackneyed expressions of sentiment. I have standardized spellings used in the various dictionaries and in most cases have settled on one common name with alternative names or spellings listed under "Other Common Names." The cross references give only the simple common name of a flower; so to find, for example, the listing for "Yellow Rose," look under "Rose, Yellow" and also scan the "Other Common Name" listings under Rose. The vast majority of botanical names listed in the appendix can be found in Bailey's *Standard Cyclopedia of Horticulture*, and I have standardized the spelling of these botanical names to correspond with Bailey's.

Adams, John Stowell. *Flora's Album, containing The Language of Flowers Poetically Expressed.* New York: Leavitt & Trow, 1848. (**A**)

The Bouquet: Containing the Poetry and Language of Flowers. By a Lady. Boston: Mussey, 1844. (**M**)

Daniels, George. *The Floral Kingdom: Its History, Sentiment and Poetry.* Chicago: Standard-Columbian, 1891. (**Da**)

Dumont, Henrietta. *The Language of Flowers. The Floral Offering: A Token of Affection and Esteem; Comprising The Language and Poetry of Flowers, with Coloured Illustrations, from Original Drawings.* Philadelphia: Bliss, 1864. (**Du**)

Edgarton [Mayo], Sarah Carter. *The Flower Vase; Containing The Language of Flowers and Their Poetic Sentiments.* Lowell: Merrill & Heywood, 1848. (**E**)

Flowers, Their Language, Poetry, and Sentiment, with Choicest Extracts from Poets, A Dictionary of the Sentiment of Every Flower, Botanical Descriptions, &c. Philadelphia: Porter & Coates, 1870. (**P**)

Greenaway, Kate. *Language of Flowers.* London: Routledge, n.d. [1884]. (**G**)

Hale, Sarah Josepha. *Flora's Interpreter: or the American Book of Flowers and Sentiments.* Boston: Marsh, Capen & Lyon 1832. (**Ha**)
——. *Flora's Interpreter, and Fortuna Flora...Revised and Enlarged Edition, with New Illustrations.* Boston: Mussey, 1865. (**Ha2**) [**Ha** and **Ha2** are identical, with the exception of those items coded **Ha2**.]

Hooper, Lucy. *The Lady's Book of Flowers and Poetry; To Which Are Added, a Botanical Introduction, a Complete Floral Dictionary; and a Chapter on Plants in Rooms.* New York: Riker, 1851. (**Ho**)

Kirtland, Mrs. C. M. *Poetry of the Flowers.* New York: Crowell, n.d. [1845]. (**K**)

The Language of Flowers; with Illustrative Poetry: To which is now first added, The Calendar of Flowers. 5th ed. Philadelphia: Lea & Blanchard, 1839. [1st ed. London: Frederick Shoberl, ed., London: Saunders & Otey, 1834.] (**Le**)

Latour, Charlotte de. *Le Langage des Fleurs,* 3rd ed. Paris: Audot, n.d. [1st ed. 1819.] (**L**)

The Language of Flowers: An Alphabet of Floral Emblems. London: Nelson, 1858. (**N**)

Osgood, Frances. *The Poetry of Flowers and Flowers of Poetry.* Philadelphia: Lippincott, 1864. (**O**)

Tyas, Robert. *The Language of Flowers; or, Floral Emblems of Thoughts, Feelings, and Sentiments.* London: Routledge, n.d. [1st ed. 1869. Tyas also wrote *The Sentiment of Flowers; or, Language of Flora.* London, 1836.] (**T**)

Waterman [Esling], Catharine H. *Flora's Lexicon: An Interpretation of The Language and Sentiment of Flowers: With an Outline of Botany, and a Poetical Introduction.* Boston: Crosby & Ainsworth, 1865. (**Wa**)

Summary of Books in the Appendix

CODE	EDITOR OR PUBLISHER	DATE
A	Adams	1848
Da	Daniels	1891
Du	Dumont	1864
E	Edgarton	1848
G	Greenaway	1884
Ha	Hale	1832
Ha2	Hale	1865
Ho	Hooper	1851
K	Kirtland	1845
L	Latour	1819
Le	Lea	1839
N	Nelson	1858
M	Mussey	1844
O	Osgood	1864
P	Porter	1870
T	Tyas	1869
Wa	Waterman	1865

FLOWER	OTHER COMMON NAME	BOTANICAL NAME	SENTIMENT	SOURCE
Abatina			fickleness	G, K, N
Abecedary			volubility	K, N
Abies, see Balsam, Pine				
Abutilon, see Indian Mallow				
Acacia, Rose	Acacia	*Acacia* (E),	chaste love, platonic love	E, Ho, L, Le, N, O, ...
		Robinia pseudacacia (T, Wa)		P, T, Wa
Acacia, Rose	Acacia	*Robinia hispida* (Da, T)	friendship	Da, Du, G, K, Le, N .
Acacia, Rose or White		*Robinia hispida* (Wa)	elegance	G, K, Ho, L, Le, Wa.
Acacia, Yellow		*Acacia farnesiana* (Ha, M)	concealed love, secret love	A, Ha, G, K, M, N
Acanthus		*Acanthus mollis* (T)	art, the arts, artifice,	A, Du, Ho, G, K, L, .
			the fine arts	Le, N, O, P, T
Acer, see Maple, Sycamore				
Achillia, see Yarrow				
Achimenes Cupreata			such worth is rare	G, K
Aconite-leaved Crowfoot, see Buttercup				
Aconitum, see Monkshood				
Acorus, see Sweet Flag				
Adder's Tongue		*Ophioglossum vulgatum* (Da)	deceit	Da
Adiantum, see Fern				
Adonis	Flos Adonis, Pheasant's	*Adonis autumnalis* (Da, T),	painful recollections, remem-	A, Da, G, Ho, K, L, .
	Eye	*Flos adonis* (Wa)	brance, sorrowful remem-	Le, N, Wa
Adonis	Pheasant's Eye		brances, sad memories	
Adoxa, see Musk Plant				
Aesculus, see Horse Chestnut				
African Marigold, see Marigold				
Agaricus, see Mushroom				
Agave, see Aloe				
Ageratum		*Ageratum mexicanum* (Da)	politeness	Da
Agnus Castus	Chaste Tree	*Vitex agnus castus* (T)	chastity	T
Agnus Castus	Chaste Tree	*Vitex agnus castus* (T)	coldness, indifference	G, K, L, N, O, T
Agnus Castus			life without love	L
Agrimony		*Agrimonia eupatoria* (T)	gratitude, thankfulness	Da, G, K, Ho, L, Le,.
		Agrimonia parviflora (Da)		
Agrimony			recognition	L
Agrostemna, see Campion				
Ailantus		*Ailantus glandulosa*	lofty aspirations	Da
Alfalfa, see Lucern				
Allspice			compassion	G, K
Almond		*Amygdalus pumila* (Da)	despair	Da
Almond Laurel, see Laurel				
Almond, Almond Tree		*Amygdalus communis* (T)	heedlessness, thoughtlessness	A, Ho, L, O, P, T
Almond, Common	Almond Tree	*Amygdalus communis* (P)	indiscretion	G, K, Le, N. P, O
Almond, Common			stupidity	G, K, N
Almond, Flowering		*Amygdalus* (H), *A. pumila* (M)	hope	G, Ha, K, M
Aloe			acute sorrow or affliction	Ho, L, N
Aloe			bitterness	K, L, T
Aloe	Agave	*Agave americana* (Da)	grief	Da, G, K, Le, N, T, Wa
Aloe			imagination	
Aloe		*Aloe* (H, M)	religious superstition	G, Ha, K, M
Aloysia, see Verbena				
Althea, see Hollyhock, Mallow			tranquility	L
Alyssum, Rock			tranquility	L
Alyssum, Sweet		*Alyssum maritimum* (Da)	merit before beauty	Da
Alyssum, Sweet		*Alyssum* (E)	worth beyond beauty	A, E, G, Ho, K, O

155

FLOWER	OTHER COMMON NAME	BOTANICAL NAME	SENTIMENT	SOURCE
Amaranth	Prince's Feather,	*Amaranthus* (E, H, P, Wa)	immortality	A, Du, E, Ha, Ho, L,
	Cockscomb			Le, N, O, P, T, Wa
Amaranth	Prince's Feather	*Amaranthus* (P)	unfading	P, T
	Cockscomb			
Amaranth	Cockscomb		affection, foppery	G, K
Amaranth, Crested	Cockscomb		singularity	Ho
Amaranth, Globe, see Globe Amaranth				
Amaranthus, see Love-Lies-Bleeding				
Amaryllis		*Formosissima* (Ha)	beautiful, but timid	Ha
Amaryllis		*Amaryllis sarniensis* (Wa),	haughtiness, pride	Da, G, Ho, K, L,
		Sprekelia formosissima (Da)		Le, N, O, T, Wa
Amaryllis			splendid beauty	G, K, N
Amaryllis			timidity	G, K, N
Ambrosia	Bitter Weed	*Ambrosia* (Ha)	love returned	G, Ha, Ho, K, N, O
Amerboa, see Sweet Sultan				
American Cowslip, see Cowslip				
American Cudweed, see Cudweed				
American Elm, see Elm				
American Laurel, see Laurel				
American Linden, see Linden				
American Sweetbriar, see Eglantine				
Amethyst			admiration	G, K
Amygdalus, see Almond				
Anagallis, see Pimpernel				
Anchusa, see Bugloss				
Andromeda			will you help me?	P
Andromeda, Marsh, see Marsh Andromeda				
Anemone	Windflower, Zephyr	*Anemone coronaria* (Da),	anticipation, expectation	Da, G, Ha, K, M, N, P
	Flower	*A. vernalis* (M),		
		A. virginiana (Ha)		
Anemone	Garden Anemone	*Anemone* (Wa)	abandonment, desertion,	A, Du, G, K, L,
			forsaken	Le, N, O, P, Wa
Anemone	Windflower	*Anemone* (E), *A. virginiana* (P)	frailty	E, P
Anemone	Field Anemone, Meadow	*Anemone pratensis* (T),	sickness	Du, G, K, L, Le, Ho, N,
	Anemone, Zephyr Flower	*Anemone virginiana* (P)		O, P
Anemone	Windflower	*A. virginiana* (P)	withered hopes	P
Anemone			your frown I defy	O
Anethum, see Fennel				
Angelica		*Angelica* (Wa),	inspiration	Da, G, Ho, K, L,
		A. archangelica (T),		Le, N, Wa
		A. atropurpurea (Da)		
Angelica			magic	K
Angrec			royalty	G, Ho, K, Le, N, O
Anthoxanthum, see Grass				
Antirrhinum, see Snapdragon				
Apium, see Parsley				
Apocynum, see Dogsbane				
Apple			temptation	G, K, N
Apple Blossom		*Pyrus* (E)	fame speaks you/him great	E, G, Ho, K, N, O
			and good	P, T, Wa
Apple Blossom		*Pyrus* (Wa), *P. malus* (Da)	preference	Da, G, K, L, Le, O
Apple Geranium, see Geranium				
Apricot		*Prunus armeniaca* (Da)	temptation	Da
Apricot Blossom			doubt	K
Aquilegia, see Columbine				

FLOWER	OTHER COMMON NAME	BOTANICAL NAME	SENTIMENT	SOURCE
Aralia, see Spikenard				
Arbor Vitae	Tree of Life	*Thuja* (Wa)	live for me	G, K, Wa
Arbor Vitae	False White Cedar	*Thuja* (Ha)	unchanging friendship	G, Ha, K, N
Arbor Vitae, American		*Thuja occidentalis* (Wa)	immortality	Wa
Arbor Vitae, American		*Thuja occidentalis* (Da)	thine till death	Da
Arbutus	Strawberry-tree		thee only do I love	K, P
Arbutus, see also Trailing Arbutus				
Arctium, see Burdock				
Arethusa		*Arethusa bulbosa* (Da)	fear	Da
Argentine			naivete	L
Aristolochia, see Dutchman's Pipe				
Armeria, see Thrift				
Arnica		*Arnica mollis* (Da)	let me heal thy grief	Da
Artemisia, see Mudwort, Mugwort, Southernwood, Wormwood				
Arum	Cuckoo Plant, Cuckoo Pint, Jack in the Pulpit, Wake Robin		ardor, zeal	G, K, Ho, L, N, O
Arum	Wake Robin	*Dracontium* (Ha)	deceit and ferocity	Ha
Arum, see Calla				
Arum, Spotted		*Arum maculatum* (T)	warmth	T
Asclepias, see Butterfly Weed				
Ash, Ash Tree		*Fraxinus* (E, P, Wa), *F. ameri-cana* (Da), *F. excelsior* (T)	grandeur	Da, Du, E, G, Ho, K, L, Le, N, P, T, Wa.
Ash, Mountain, see Mountain Ash				
Ash-leaved Trumpet Flower, see Trumpet Flower				
Asiatic Ranunculus, see Buttercup				
Asparagus		*Asparagus officinalis* (Da)	emulation	Da
Aspen Tree			fear	K
Aspen Tree			lamentation	A, G, Ho, K, N
Aspen, Aspen Tree		*Populus tremuloides* (Da), *P. tremulus* (Wa)	excessive sensibility	Da, M, Wa
Aspen, Quaking			frivolity	L
Asphodel		*Tofieldia palustris* (Wa)	my regrets follow you to the grave.	G, Ho, K, L, Le, N, O, T, Wa
Asphodel		*Asphodelus luteus* (Da)	remembered beyond the tomb	Da
Aster	Catesby's Starwort, China Aster, China Starwort, Michaelmas Daisy, Starwort	*Aster chinensis* (P), *A. grandiflorus* (Wa), *A. tradescanti* (T)	afterthought	G, Ho, K, Le, O, P, T, Wa
Aster	Starwort	*Aster* (E)	beauty in retirement	E
Aster	Michaelmas Daisy, American Starwort	*Aster corymbosus* (Da)	cheerfulness in old age	Da, G, K, Ho
Aster	Michaelmas Daisy		farewell	A, G, K
Aster	American Starwort	*Aster tradescantii* (H)	welcome to a stranger	A, G, Ha, Ho, K, O...
Aster, China	China Starwort	*Aster chinensis* (Ha, M, P, T)	love of variety, variety, variety is charming	Du, G, Ha, Ho, K, L, Le, M, N, P, T
Aster, China	China Starwort	*Aster chinensis* (Wa)	variety of charms	Wa
Aster, China		*Aster* (E)	your sentiments meet with a return	E
Aster, China, Double		*Callistephus chinensis* (Da)	bounty	Da
Aster, China, Double			I partake/share your sentiments	G, K, N
Aster, China, Single		*Callistephus chinensis* (Da)	I will think of it	Da, G, K, N
Aster, Large-Flowered			ulterior motive	L

157

FLOWER	OTHER COMMON NAME	BOTANICAL NAME	SENTIMENT	SOURCE
Atropa, see Nightshade				
Auricula	Lilac Polyanthus	*Primula auricula* (E, P)	confidence	E, G, Ho, K, N, O, P
Auricula		*Primula auricula* (Da, Wa)	painting	A, Da, G, Ho, K, N, O, Wa
Auricula	Polyanthus	*Primula auricula* (Ha, P)	pride of newly acquired fortune, pride of riches	G, K, Ha, N, P
Auricula, Scarlet			avarice	G, K, N
Auricula, Scarlet		*Primula auricula* (H)	pride	Ha
Auricula, Scarlet		*Primula auricula* (M)	wealth is not happiness	M
Auricula, Yellow			splendor	K
Austrian Rose, see Rose				
Autumn Crocus, see Meadow Saffron				
Autumnal Leaves, see Leaves				
Avena, see Oats				
Azalea	Indian Azalea	*Azalea indica* (Wa)	romance	A, Wa
Azalea		*Azalea indica* (Da)	temperance	Da, G, Ho, K, N
Azalea			your blush has won me	O
Azalea, see Honeysuckle				
Baccharis, see Groundsel Tree				
Bachelor's Button, see Corn Flower, Lychnis				
Ballota, see Hoarhound				
Balm		*Melissa officinalis* (T)	pleasantry	O, T
Balm		*Melissa officinalis* (Ha)	social intercourse	Ha
Balm	Rose Balm	*Melissa nepeta* (E)	sweets of social intercourse	E
Balm	Sweet Balm	*Melissa officinalis* (Da)	charms	Da
Balm		*Melissa officinalis* (M)	sympathy	K, M
Balm of Gilead	Balm of Judea		cure, healing	Du, G, K, L, Le, O, T
Balm of Gilead		*Populus balsamifera* (E, P)	I am cured	E, P
Balm of Gilead			relief	G, K, P
Balm of Gilead		*Populus candicans* (Da)	sympathetic feeling	Da
Balm, Gentle			joking	Du, Le
Balm, Gentle	Lemon Balm		pleasantry	G, K, L, O
Balm, Molucca	Shell Flower	*Moluccella laevis* (Da)	you excite my curiosity	Da
Balm, see Monarda				
Balsam	Balsam Fir	*Abies balsamea* (Da)	health	Da
Balsam, Balsamine	Touch Me Not, Yellow Balsam	*Impatiens* (Ha, M, P, Wa), *I. balsamina* (Da), *I. nolitangere* (T)	impatience	Da, Du, E, G, K, Ha, Ho, L, Le, M, O, P, T, Wa
Balsam, Red	Impatiens, Touch Me Not		impatient resolve	G, K, N
Balsam, Red	Impatiens, Touch Me Not		touch me not	G, K
Barberry	Berberry	*Berberis* (E, P), *B. vulgaris* (Da, T, Wa)	ill temper, petulance, sharpness, sharpness of temper, sour disposition, sourness, tartness	Da, Du, E, G, Ho, K, Le, O, P, T
Bartonia, Golden		*Mentzelia lindleyi* (Da)	does he possess riches?	Da
Basil	Sweet Basil	*Ocimum basilicum* (Da)	good wishes	Da
Basil	Sweet Basil	*Ocimum basilicum* (P, T)	hate, hatred	Du, G, Ho, K, L, Le, O, P, T
Basket Osier, see Osier				
Bass-wood, see Linden				
Batatas, see Sweet Potato				
Bay, see Laurel				
Bayberry	Wax Myrtle	*Myrica cerifera* (Da)	I respect thy tears	Da

158

FLOWER	OTHER COMMON NAME	BOTANICAL NAME	SENTIMENT	SOURCE
Bayberry			I will enlighten you	O
Bayberry	Wax Myrtle	*Myrica cerifera* (Wa)	instruction	O, Wa
Bearded Crepis			protection	G, K, Ho, O
Bear's Breech			art	O
Bed Straw	Scratch Weed	*Galium verum* (T)	hardness	T
Bee Ophrys, see Ophrys				
Bee Orchis, see Orchis				
Beech		*Fagus sylvatica* (Da)	lovers' tryst	Da
Beech		*Fagus sylvatica* (Wa)	wedded love	Wa
Beech Tree			grandeur	Ho
Beech, Beech Tree		*Fagus sylvatica* (T)	prosperity	Du, G, K, L, Le, T
Begonia		*Begonia discolor* (Da)	deformity	Da, K
Belladonna			silence	G, K, N
Belladonna			hush!	K
Belle of the Day or Night, see Daphne				
Bellflower	Canterbury Bell	*Campanula medium* (P)	acknowledgement	G, K, N, P
Bellflower	Bluebell, Bluebell of Scot-land, Canterbury Bell, Harebell, Pyramidal Bellflower	*Campanula* (E, P,) *C. pyramidalis* (T), *C. rotundifolis* (Wa)	constancy	A, E, G, Ho, K, L, Le, N, O, P, T, Wa
Bellflower	Bluebell of Scotland, Harebell	*Campanula rotundifolia* (Da)	a constant heart, constancy in love	Da, P
Bellflower	Harebell		delicate and lonely as this flower	Ho, O
Bellflower	Canterbury Bell, Pyramidal Bellflower	*Campanula medium* (Da, Ha, P, Wa)	gratitude	A, Da, G, Ha, Ho, K, N, O, P, Wa
Bellflower	Bluebell of Scotland, Harebell	*Campanula rotundifolia* (Ha, M)	grief	G, Ha, K, M
Bellflower	Bluebell		sorrowful regret	G, K
Bellflower	Bluebell, Bluebell of Scotland, Campanula, Harebell, Pyramidal Bellflower	*Hyacinthus non-scriptus* (Wa)	submission	G, K, Wa
Bellis, see Daisy				
Belvedere	Kochia, Summer Cypress		I declare (war) against you	G, Ho, K, L, N, O
Berberis, Berberry, see Barberry				
Betony			surprise	G, Ho, K, N, O
Betula, see Birch				
Bignonia, see Jasmine, Trumpet Flower				
Bilberry, see Whortleberry				
Bindweed, see Convolvulus				
Birch		*Betula* (E), *B. alba* (Wa), *B. lenta* (Da), *B. pendula* (T)	elegance, gracefulness	Da, E, Ho, O, T, Wa
Birch			meekness	G, K, N
Bird Cherry, see Cherry				
Birdfoot Trefoil, see Clover				
Bitter Cress, see Cardamine				
Bitter Weed, see Ambrosia				
Bittersweet Nightshade, see Nightshade				
Black Bryony		*Tamus communis* (T)	be my support	T
Black Hoarhound, see Hoarhound				
Black Mulberry Tree, see Mulberry				
Black Poplar, see Poplar				
Black Spruce, see Pine				
Black Walnut, see Walnut				
Blackthorn	Thorns	*Crategus coccinea* (Da), *Prunus spinosa* (T)	difficulty	Da, G, Ho, K, L, N, O, T

FLOWER	OTHER COMMON NAME	BOTANICAL NAME	SENTIMENT	SOURCE
Bladdernut	Bladder Senna	*Staphylea pinnata* (T)	amusement, frivolity,	Du, G, Ho, K, L Le,
			frivolous amusement	N, O, T
Bladdernut		*Staphylea trifolia* (Da)	trifling character	Da
Bladdernut				
Blaeberry			ingenuous simplicity	N
Blue Convolvulus Minor, see Morning Glory				
Blue Hyacinth, see Hyacinth				
Blue Periwinkle, see Periwinkle				
Blue Salvia, see Salvia				
Blue Violet, see Violet				
Bluebell, see Bellflower				
Bluebottle, see Corn Flower				
Blue-flowered Greek Valerian, see Valerian				
Bluet, see Houstonia				
Bonus Henricus, see Goosefoot				
Borage		*Borago officinalis* (Da, T)	abruptness, bluntness, rudeness	A, Da, Du, G, Ho, K, L . Le, N, O, T
Borage			roughness of manner	A, Ho, O
Bouncing Bess		*Saponaria officinalis* (Da)	intrusion	Da
Bouquet of Flowers			gallantry, politeness	T
Box			constancy	Ha, P, Wa
Box		*Buxus* (Ha, P, Wa)		
Box	Dwarf Box, Boxwood	*Buxus* (E, P, Wa),	stoicism	Da, Du, E, G, Ho,
		B. sempervirens (Da, T)		K, L, Le, M, N,
		B. suffruticosa (M)		O, P, T, Wa
Bramble	Common Bramble	*Rubus fruticosus* (T)	envy	Du, G, Ho, K, L, Le, N, O, T
Bramble			lowliness	G, K, N
Bramble			remorse	A, G, Ho, K, N
Branch of Currant, see Currant				
Branch of Thorn, see Thorn				
Brassica, see Cabbage				
Bridal Rose, see Rose				
Briza, see Grass, Trembling				
Broken Corn, see Corn				
Broken Straw, see Straw				
Bromelia Ananas, see Pineapple				
Broom	Furze, Gorse, Whin			
Broom	Furze, Gorse, Whin		anger	G, K, N
Broom	Furze	*Genista* (Ha, P), *Genista*	ardor	Du, Le
Broom		*tinctoria* (Da)	humility	Da, Du, Ha, K, Le, N, P
Broom	Furze		neatness	K, L, N, O, P
Broom			mirth	O
Broom Corn, see Sorghum				
Browallia		*Browallia cerulea* (Da),	can you bear poverty?	Da, G, K
		B. jamisonii (G, K)		
Bryony		*Bryonia diocia* (Wa)	prosperity	Ho, O, Wa
Buckbean		*Menyanthes trifoliata* (T)	calm, calmness,	Du, G, Ho, K, L, Le, N,.
			calm repose, repose	O, T
Buckbean			flattery's smile	O
Buckeye, see Horse Chestnut				
Bugloss	Anchusa		falsehood	Du, G, Ho, K, L, Le, N,.
				O, T
Bugloss		*Anchusa officinalis* (Da)	hypocrisy	Da

160

FLOWER	OTHER COMMON NAME	BOTANICAL NAME	SENTIMENT	SOURCE
Bulrush	Rush	*Juncus conglomeratus* (T)	docility	Du, G, Ho, K, L, Le,. N, O, T
Bulrush	Reed	*Scirpus lacustris* (Da)	indecision	Da
Bulrush			indiscretion	Du, G, K, Le
Bundles of Reeds, see Reed				
Buphthalmum, see Daisy				
Burdock		*Arctium* (E, N), *A. lappa/bardana* (T)	importunity, inconvenience	E, G, K, L, N, N, T
Burdock		*Lappa major* (Da)	proximity undesirable	Da
Burdock			touch me not	Du, G, K, Le, N
Burgundy Rose, see Rose				
Burning Nettle, see Nettle				
Burr			you weary me	K, L
Burr, see Clotbur				
Buttercup	Crowfoot, King-Cup, Ranunculus		childishness	G, Ho, K, N.
Buttercup	Crowfoot, King-Cup	*Ranunculus acris* (Da)	distrust	Da
Buttercup	Ranunculus		I am dazzled by your charms	N
Buttercup	Crowfoot, King-Cup	*Ranunculus acris* (Wa), *R. bulbosus* (Da), *R. sceleratus* (T)	ingratitude	Du, G, Ho, K, L, Le,. N, O, T, Wa
Buttercup	Crowfoot, King-Cup	*Ranunculus acris* (Ha, P)	memories of childhood	Ha, P
Buttercup	Crowfoot, King-Cup	*Ranunculus* (E, P), *R. acris* (Ha, M, P)	riches, desire of riches, I wish I was rich, wealth	E, G, Ha, K, M, N,. O, P
Buttercup	Asiatic Ranunculus		you are radiant with charms	A, Du, G, K, L, Le, O
Buttercup	Garden Ranunculus		you are rich in attractions	G, Ho, K, N, O.
Buttercup, Aconite-leaved	Aconite-leaved Crowfoot, Fair Maids of France		luster	G, Ho, K, O.
Butterfly Orchis, see Orchis				
Butterfly Weed	Asclepias, Swallowwort		cure for heartache	G, Ho, K, N, O
Butterfly Weed	Asclepias, Swallowwort		let me go	G, K
Butterfly Weed	Asclepias, Swallowwort		medicine	Ho, O
Buxus, see Box				
Cabbage		*Brassica* (T)	gain, profit	G, Ho, K, L, N, O, T
Cabbage Rose, see Rose				
Cacalia		*Cacalia coccinea* (Da)	adulation	Da, G, K
Cactus, see also Cereus, Prickly Pear				
Cactus, Common	Indian Fig		I burn	Ho, O
Cactus, Serpentine		*Cactus serpentinus* (T)	horror	O, T
Cactus, Snake		*Cereus flagelliformis* (Da)	you terrify me	Da
Cactus, Virginia			horror	Le
Calceolaria			I offer you pecuniary assis- tance, I offer you my fortune	K
Calceolaria		*Calceolaria hybrida* (Da)	novelty	Da
Calendula, see Marigold				
Calla	Calla Ethiopica	*Arum* (E), *A. ethiopica* (M)	feminine modesty	E, Ho, M, O
Calla	Calla Ethiopica	*Arum ethiopica* (Ha), *Calla ethiopica* (P)	magnificent beauty	G, Ha, K, N, P
Calla		*Calla ethiopica* (P)	modesty	P
Calla Lily		*Richardia ethiopica* (Da)	feminine beauty	Da
Callistephus, see Aster				
Calycanthus	Carolina Allspice	*Calycanthus floridus* (Da, Ha)	benevolence	Da, G, Ha, Ho, K, N, O, P.

161

FLOWER	OTHER COMMON NAME	BOTANICAL NAME	SENTIMENT	SOURCE
Calycanthus	Carolina Allspice	*Calycanthus floridus* (P)	compassion	N, P
Calystegia, see Convolvulus				
Camellia	White Camellia	*Camellia japonica* (Da, M)	perfect loveliness	Da, G, K, M
Camellia Japonica	Rose of Japan		supreme loveliness	P
Camellia Japonica	Red Camellia Japonica	*Camellia japonica* (Ha)	unpretending excellence	G, Ha, K, N
Camellia	Japan Rose	*Camellia japonica* (Wa)	my destiny is in your hands	Wa
Campanula, see Bellflower				
Camphire			fragrance	K
Campion, Rose		*Agrostemma githago* (Ha)	love's messenger	Ha
Campion, Rose			only deserve my love	G, K, N
Campion, Rose			you are without pretension	Ho, L, O
Canary Grass, see Grass				
Candytuft		*Iberis umbelleta* (Da)	architecture	Da, Ho
Candytuft	Everblooming Candytuft	*Iberis* (E, M, P),	indifference	A, E, G, Ho, K, L, M,
		I. semperflorens (T)		N, O, P, T
Canna, see Reed				
Cannabis, see Hemp				
Canterbury Bell, see Bellflower				
Cape Jasmine, see Jasmine				
Cape Marigold, see Marigold				
Cardamine	Bitter Cress	*Cardamine hirsuta* (Da)	infatuation	Da
Cardamine			paternal error	G, K, Ho, N, O
Cardinal Flower		*Lobelia* (E, P),	distinction	E, G, Ha, Ho, K, N, O,
		L. cardinalis (Ha, Wa)		P, Wa
Cardinal Flower		*Lobelia cardinalis* (Da)	preferment	Da
Carduus, see Thistle				
Carion Flower, see Stapelia				
Carnation, see Pink				
Carolina Jasmine, see Jasmine				
Carolina Rose, see Rose				
Carolina Syringa, see Syringa				
Carthamus, see Saffron				
Carya, see Hickory				
Caryophyllus, see Clove				
Castanea, see Chestnut Tree				
Catalpa Tree			beware of the coquette	Ho, O
Catchfly		*Silene* (Ha)	artifice	Ha, M
Catchfly		*Silene* (Ha, P),	pretended love	Ha, M, N, P
		S. pennsylvanica (M)		
Catchfly		*Silene* (E, P)	snare, a snare	E, G, K, Le, N, O, P
Catchfly	Red Catchfly		youthful love	G, Ho, K, N
Catchfly, White			betrayed	G, K, N
Catesby's Starwort, see Aster				
Cattleya	Orchid		mature charms	K
Cattleya, Pinelia	Orchid, Pinelia Cattleya		matronly grace	K
Cedar			constancy	N
Cedar		*Juniperus* (M)	I think of thee	M
Cedar	Juniper		protection	O, P
Cedar		*Juniperus* (E), *J. virginia* (P)	spiritual strength	E, P
Cedar			strength	G, Ho, K, N, O, P
Cedar	Red Cedar, Virginia Juniper	*Juniperus* (Ha)	think of me	Ha
Cedar Leaf			I live for thee	G, K, N
Cedar of Lebanon			incorruptible	G, Ho, K, N, O
Celandine			deceptive hopes	P

FLOWER	OTHER COMMON NAME	BOTANICAL NAME	SENTIMENT	SOURCE
Celandine		*Chelidonium majus* (Da)	future happiness	Da
Celandine	Lesser Celandine		joys to come	G, K, N, P
Celosia, see Cockscomb				
Centaurea Cyanus, see Corn Flower				
Centaury, see Sweet Sultan				
Cereus, see also Cactus				
Cereus, Creeping			horror	G, Ho, K, O
Cereus, Creeping			modest genius	G, K
Cereus, Night-blooming	Night-blooming Cereus	*Cactus grandiflorus* (Da, Wa)	transient beauty	Da, G, Ho, K, N, O, Wa
Cetraria, see Moss				
Chamomile		*Anthemis nobilis* (Ha, M, P)	energy in adversity	Du, G, Ha, Ho, K, M, N, O, P
Chamomile		*Anthemis nobilis* (Da)	mercy	Da
Champignon, see Mushroom				
Chaste Tree, see Agnus Castus				
Checkered Lily, see Fritillaria				
Cheiranthus, see Wallflower				
Chelidonium, see Celandine				
Cherry Blossom		*Prunus* (E)	spiritual beauty	E, Ho, O
Cherry Laurel				
Cherry Tree, White			deception	G, N
Cherry, Bird		*Prunus padus* (Wa)	hope	Ho, O, Wa
Cherry, Cherry Tree	White Cherry Tree	*Prunus cerasus* (T, Wa)	education, good education	G, K, L, Le, N, O, T, Wa
Chervil, Garden			sincerity	G, Ho, K, O
Chestnut		*Castanea vesca* (Da)	deceptive appearances	Da
Chestnut Tree		*Castanea vesca* (T)	do/render me justice	G, K, L, Le, N, O, T
Chestnut, Chestnut Tree			luxury	G, N
Chichorium, see Chicory				
Chickweed			rendezvous	G, K, N
Chickweed		*Stellaria media* (Da)	star of my existence	Da
Chickweed, Mouse-eared			ingenuous simplicity	G, Ho, K, N, O
Chicory	Succory	*Chichorium intybus* (Da, T)	frugality, prudent economy	Da, G, K, L, Le, N, T
China Aster, China Starwort, see Aster				
China Pink, see Pink				
China Rose, see Rose				
Chinese Chrysanthemum, see Chrysanthemum				
Chinese Primrose, see Primrose				
Chirraphila, see Evergreen				
Chorozema Varium			you have many lovers	K
Christmas Rose			relieve my anxiety	G, K
Christmas Rose, see also Rose				
Chrysanthemum		*Chrysanthemum carinatum* (Da)	slighted affections	Da
Chrysanthemum, Chinese	Xeranthemum		cheerfulness under adversity	G, Ho, K, N, O
Chrysanthemum, Chinese		*Chrysanthemum indicum* (Wa)	loveliness and cheerfulness	Wa
Chrysanthemum, Red		*Chrysanthemum indicum* (M)	I love	G, K, M, N
Chrysanthemum, White			truth	G, K, N
Chrysanthemum, Yellow		*Chrysanthemum* (E)	a heart left to desolation	E
Chrysanthemum, Yellow			slighted love	G, K, N
Cichorium, see Endive				
Cigridia, see Tiger Flower				
Cineraria		*Cineraria amelloides* (Da)	always delightful	Da, K
Cinquefoil		*Potentilla* (T)	beloved daughter	Le, T

163

FLOWER	OTHER COMMON NAME	BOTANICAL NAME	SENTIMENT	SOURCE
Cinquefoil			darling girl	L
Cinquefoil		*Potentilla* (E)	love, constant but hopeless	E
Cinquefoil			maternal affection	G, K, N
Cinquefoil			parental love	A, O
Circa, see Enchanter's Nightshade				
Cistus	Rock Rose		popular favor	O
Cistus	Rock Rose		safety	T
Cistus, Gum			I shall die tomorrow	G, K, N
Citron			estrangement	Du
Citron			ill-natured beauty	G, K
Citron		*Citrus medica* (Da)	marriage	Da
Citronella			sorrow	L
Citrus, see Citron, Lemon, Orange				
Clarkia			the variety of your conversation delights me	K
Clematis	Virgin's Bower	*Clematis virginiana* (P, Wa)	artifice	A, Ho, K, L, Le, P, O, T, Wa
Clematis	Virgin's Bower	*Clematis viorna* (Ha), *Clematis virginiana* (Da)	filial affection, filial love	Da, G, Ha, K, N
Clematis	Virgin's Bower	*Clematis* (E), *Clematis virginiana* (Ha, M, P)	mental beauty/excellence	E, G, Ha, K, M, N, P
Clematis	Traveler's Joy		safety	G, K, N
Clematis, English	Traveler's Joy	*Clematis vitalba* (Wa)	traveler's joy	A, Wa
Clematis, Evergreen			poverty	G, K, N
Clianthus			self-seeking	K
Clianthus			worldliness	K
Clianthus, see Glory Flower				
Climbing Cobaea, see Cobaea				
Clotbur	Burr	*Xanthium strumarium* (Da)	detraction	Da
Clotbur	Burr, Xanthium		pertinacity, rudeness	G, K, L, Le, N
Clove	Clove-tree, Gillyflower	*Caryophyllus aromaticus* (T)	dignity	G, K, L, Le, N, T
Clover			I promise	P
Clover	Purple or Red Clover	*Trifolium pratense* (Da)	industry	Da, G, K, N
Clover	Purple or Red Clover, Trefoil	*Trifolium pratense* (Wa)	providence, provident	G, Ho, K, O, Wa
Clover	Trefoil, Birdfoot Trefoil	*Lotos, L. corniculatus* (Wa)	revenge	G, Ho, K, N, O, Wa
Clover, Four-leaved	Four-leaved Clover		be mine	G, K
Clover, White	Shamrock	*Trifolium repens* (Da)	lightheartedness	Da, G, K, N
Clover, White			promise	K
Clover, White			think of me	G, K
Cobaea	Climbing Cobaea	*Cobaea scandens* (Da)	gossip	A, Da, G, Ho, N, O
Cockscomb, see also Amaranth		*Celosia cristata* (Da)	foppery	Da, G, K
Colchicum, see Meadow Saffron				
Coltsfoot	Sweet-scented Coltsfoot, Sweet-scented Tussilago	*Nardosmia palmata* (Da), *Tussilago fragrans* (T, Wa)	justice to you, you shall have justice	Da, Du, G, Ho, K, L, Le, N, O, T, Wa
Coltsfoot	Sweet-scented Coltsfoot, Sweet-scented Tussilago	*Tussilago farfara* (Wa)	maternal care	Ho, Wa
Columbine		*Aquilegia* (Ha)	desertion	A, Du, Ha
Columbine		*Aquilegia* (Wa), *A. vulgaris* (T), *A. canadensis* (Da)	folly	Da, G, Ho, K, L, Le, N, O, Wa
Columbine		*Aquilegia* (E, M)	I cannot give thee up	E, M
Columbine, Purple			resolution	N
Columbine, Purple			resolved to win	G, K
Columbine, Red			anxious, trembling	G, K, N

FLOWER	OTHER COMMON NAME	BOTANICAL NAME	SENTIMENT	SOURCE
Common Almond, see Almond				....
Common Bramble, see Bramble				....
Common Cactus, see Cactus....................				....
Common Fumitory, see Fumitory....................				....
Common Laurel in Flower, see Laurel....................				....
Common Milfoil, see Yarrow....................				....
Common Reed, see Reed....................				....
Common Stramonium, see Datura....................				....
Convallaria, see Lily of the Valley....................				....
Convolvulus....................			bonds	G, K, N ....
Convolvulus....................			dangerous insinuation................	Ho, O
Convolvulus....................	Small/White Bindweed	Calystegia sepium (Wa), ... Convolvulus (E, P), C. arvensis (T)	humility	E, G, K, L, N, O, P, .. T, Wa....................
Convolvulus	Great Bindweed		importunity	G, K, N ....
Convolvulus....................	Great Bindweed		insinuation	G, K, N ....
Convolvulus....................	Bindweed, Night Convolvulus	Convolvulus (P), C. minor (G, K)	night	A, G, Ho, K, L, Le.... N, O, P.
Convolvulus....................	Small Bindweed....................		obstinacy....................	Ho, O
Convolvulus....................	Sea Bindweed....................	Calystegia soldanella (Wa)........	uncertainty	N, Wa....................
Convolvulus....................	Pink Bindweed	Convolvulus (Ha)....................	worth sustained by affection	G, Ha, K ....
Convolvulus				
Convolvulus Major	Great Bindweed....................		extinguished hopes	G, Ho, K, N, O........
Convolvulus, Field....................	Field Bindweed....................		captivation	Wa....................
Coral Honeysuckle, see Honeysuckle....................				
Corallorhiza, see Dragon's Claw....................				
Corchorus		Corchorus japonicus (M)............	impatient of absence....................	A, G, Ho, K, M, O....
Coreopsis....................	Coreopsis Arkansa	Coreopsis (E), C. tinctoria (Ha, P)	always cheerful....................	E, G, Ha, K, N, P ....
Coreopsis....................		Coreopsis tinctoria (Da)	happy at all times	Da....................
Coreopsis....................		Coreopsis arkansa (M)	love at first sight....................	A, G, Ho, K, M, N, O
Coriander....................		Coriandrum (E, P), C. sativum (T)	concealed merit, hidden merit or worth	E, G, Ho, K, L, Le, ... N, O, P, T....................
Coriander....................		Coriandrum sativum (Da)	merit....................	Da....................
Corn....................	Indian Corn, Maize	Zea Mays (E, P, Wa)	abundance, plenty, riches	Du, E, G, Ho, K, Le.. N, O, P, Wa ....
Corn Bottle, see Corn Flower				
Corn Cockle	Rose Campion		gentility....................	G, K
Corn Cockle	Rose Campion	Agrostemma githago (Da)............	worth above beauty	Da....................
Corn Flower	Blue Bottle, Corn Bottle, ... Bachelor's Button	Centaurea cyanus (T, Wa)........	delicacy....................	G, Ho, K, L, Le, N,... O, P, T, Wa....................
Corn Flower	Blue Bottle, Corn Bottle, ... Bachelor's Button.	Centaurea cyanus (Da)	single blessedness....................	Da....................
Corn Poppy, see Poppy....................				
Corn Straw....................			agreement	G, K
Corn, Broken			quarrel....................	G, K
Cornel Tree, see Dogwood....................				
Cornus, see Dogwood....................				
Coronilla	Coronella	Coronilla glauca (Da)	success crown your wishes	Da, G, Ho, K, N, O...
Corylus, see Hazel				
Cosmelia Subra			the charm of a blush	K
Cotton Plant....................		Gossypium herbaceum (Da)........	greatness	Da....................
Cowslip		Primula veris (T)....................	early joys	T....................
Cowslip		Dodecatheon (E)	native grace	E....................
Cowslip			pensiveness....................	Du, G, Ho, K, N, O...

FLOWER	OTHER COMMON NAME	BOTANICAL NAME	SENTIMENT	SOURCE
Cowslip	American Cowslip	*Dodecatheon* (P), *D. meadia* (Ha)	winning grace	G, Ha, K, N, P
Cowslip		*Dodecatheon* (P)	youthful beauty	K, P
Cowslip, American			divine beauty	G, K
Cowslip, American		*Dodecatheon media* (T)	you are my angel	T
Cowslip, American		*Primula veris* (Wa)	you are my divinity	Du, G, Ho, Le, N, Wa
Crab Blossom			ill nature	K
Crab Tree Blossom, Siberian			deeply interesting	Ho, O
Cranberry			cure for heartache	Du, G, K, N
Cranberry		*Oxycoccus* (Wa), *O. palustris* (Da)	hardihood, hardiness	Da, Ho, O
Crane's Bill			envy	N
Crape Myrtle		*Lagerstroemia indica* (Da)	eloquence	Da
Crataegus, see Hawthorn				
Crategus, see Blackthorn				
Creeping Willow, see Willow				
Cress			power	G, K
Cress			resolution	Le
Cress			stability	G, K, N
Crested Iris, see Iris				
Crimson Glory Flower, see Glory Flower				
Crimson Polyanthus, see Polyanthus				
Crocus			abuse not	G, K, N
Crocus	Saffron, Spring Crocus	*Crocus* (P, Wa), *C. vernus* (Da), *C. officinalis* (M),	cheerfulness	A, Da, Ho, K, M, O, P, Wa
Crocus	Saffron	*Crocus sativus* (T)	do not deceive yourselves	T
Crocus	Saffron		mirth	G, Ho, K, N, O
Crocus			impatience	K
Crocus		*Crocus vernus* (T)	pleasures of hope	T
Crocus			smiles	A
Crocus			youth	Du
Crocus	Spring Crocus	*Crocus* (Ha)	youthful gladness	G, K, Ha, N
Cross of Jerusalem			devotion	A, Ho, O
Crowfoot, see Buttercup				
Crown Imperial		*Fritillaria imperialis* (Da, T)	imperial power	Da, T
Crown Imperial	Fritillaria, Imperial Montague		majesty	G, K, Ho, N, O
Crown Imperial	Imperial Montague	*Fritillaria imperialis* (P)	power	G, K, Ho, L, Le, N, O, P
Crown Imperial		*Fritillaria imperialis* (Ha2, P)	pride of birth	A, Ha2, P
Crown Imperial		*Fritillaria imperialis* (Ha)	pride of riches	Ha
Crown of Roses, see Roses				
Crowsbill			envy	G, K
Cuckoo Plant, Cuckoo Pint, see Arum				
Cucumber	Squirting Cucumber	*Momordica elaterium* (T)	criticism	L, N, T
Cucumber, Squirting			critic	Ho, O
Cucurbita, see Gourd				
Cudweed	American Cudweed		never-ceasing remembrance	G, K, N
Cuphea		*Cuphea viscosissima* (Da)	impatience	Da
Currant			thy frown will kill me	G, K
Currant, Branch of			you please all	Da, G, Ho, K, N, O
Cuscuta, see Dodder				
Cyclamen		*Cyclamen* (Wa), *Cyclamen persicum* (Da)	diffidence	Da, G, Ho, K, O, Wa
Cydonia, see Quince				
Cypress			death	A, G, K
Cypress		*Cupressus sempervirens* (Ha, P)	despair	Ha, Ho, O, P

FLOWER	OTHER COMMON NAME	BOTANICAL NAME	SENTIMENT	SOURCE
Cypress		*Cupressus* (E)	disappointed hopes	E
Cypress		*Cupressus sempervirens* (P, Wa)	mourning	Du, G, K, L, Le, O, P, Wa
Cypress		*Taxodium distichum* (Da)	sorrow	Da, L
Cypress and Marigold, see Marigold				
Cypress Tree			death and eternal sorrow	Ho, O
Cypress Vine, see Ipomoea				
Cypripedium, see Lady's Slipper				
Cytisus, see Laburnum				
Daffodil		*Narcissus major* (Wa) *N. pseudo-narcissus* (Da)	chivalry	Da, Wa
Daffodil	False Narcissus		deceitful hope	Ho, O
Daffodil			regard	G, K
Daffodil			self-love	Le
Daffodil		*Narcissus major* (Ha)	uncertainty	Ha
Daffodil			unrequited love	K, P
Dahlia		*Dahlia variabilis* (Da)	dignity	Da
Dahlia		*Dahlia* (E, Ha, M, P)	elegance and dignity	E, Ha, M, P
Dahlia		*Dahlia* (Wa)	forever thine	Wa
Dahlia			heartless beauty	O
Dahlia			instability	G, Ho, K, O
Dahlia		*Dahlia superflua* (T)	my gratitude exceeds your care	T
Dahlia			pomp	K
Daily Rose, see Rose				
Daisies, Wreath of			I will think of it	T
Daisy	Marguerite, White Daisy	*Bellis* (Wa), *B. perennis* (T)	innocence	A, Du, Ho, L, Le, N, O, T, Wa
Daisy	Marguerite	*Bellis* (E, Ha, M, P), *B. perennis* (Da)	innocence and beauty, beauty and innocence	Da, E, Ha, M, P
Daisy			innocence and hope	G, K
Daisy	Marguerite des Pres		reverie	L
Daisy, Double			participation	Ho
Daisy, Garden	Double Marguerite, Small Double Daisy		I partake/reciprocate/share your affections/sentiments	Du, G, K, L, Le, O, T
Daisy, Ox Eye			obstacle	Ho, O
Daisy, Ox Eye		*Buphthalmum* (Ha)	patience	G, Ha, K
Daisy, Ox Eye			token, a token	N
Daisy, Parti-colored			beauty	G, K, N
Daisy, Red			unconscious	N
Daisy, Wild	White Daisy		I will think of it	Du, G, K, Le, N, O
Dame Violet, see Violet				
Dame's Violet, see Queen's Rocket				
Dandelion		*Leontodon* (E), *L. taraxacum* (Ha, P)	coquetry	A, E, Ha, P
Dandelion			depart	K
Dandelion		*Leontodon taraxacum* (P, T, Wa)	oracle, rustic oracle, love's oracle	Du, G, Ho, K, L, Le, N, O, P, T, Wa
Dandelion		*Taraxacum dens-leonis* (Da)	youthful recollections	Da
Daphne	Belle of the Day, Mezereon, Spurge Laurel	*Daphne laureola* (T), *D. odora*(P), *Leontodon taraxacum* (M)	coquetry	Du, L, Le, M, P, T
Daphne	Mezereon, Spurge Laurel	*Daphne laureola* (T), *D. mezereum* (Wa)	desire to please, I desire to please	Du, G, Ho, K, L, Le, N, T, Wa
Daphne			glory	K

FLOWER	OTHER COMMON NAME	BOTANICAL NAME	SENTIMENT	SOURCE
Daphne			immortality	K
Daphne	Mezereon		love in a snow wreath	O
Daphne	Daphne Odora	*Daphne odorata* (Da)	sweets to the sweet	Da, Ho, O
Daphne	Belle of the Night,	*Daphne odora* (Ha)	timidity	Ha, L
	Mezereon			
Daphne Odora			painting the lily	G, K, N
Dark China Rose, see Rose				
Dark Geranium, see Geranium				
Darnel	Ray Grass, Tares	*Lolium perenne* (Da),	vice	Da, G, Ho, K, L, N,
		L. temulentus (T)		O, T
Datura	Stramonium, Thorn Apple	*Datura* (Wa),	deceitful charms	Da, Du, G, Ho, K, L,
		D. stramonium (Da, T)		Le, N, O, P, T, Wa
Datura	Common Stramonium		disguise	A, N, O
Datura	Stramonium, Thorn Apple	*Datura stramonium* (Ha)	I dreamed of thee	Ha
Datura	Stramonium, Thorn Apple		deceit	L
Day Lily	Yellow Day Lily	*Hemerocallis fulva* (Da)	coquetry	Da, Du, G, K, Ho, Le,
				N, O
Dead Leaves, see Leaves				
Deadly Nightshade, see Nightshade				
Deep Red Rose, see Rose				
Delphinium, see Larkspur				
Dew Plant	Fig Marigold	*Mesembryanthemum*	serenade, a serenade	E, G, Ha, Ho, K, M, N, O
		(E, Ha, M)		
Dianthus, see Pink, Sweet William				
Dictamnus, see Fraxinella				
Digitalis, see Foxglove				
Dionea, see Venus's Flytrap				
Diosma			uselessness	N
Diosma			your single elegance charms me	K
Diospyros, see Ebenaster, Persimmon				
Diplademia Crassinoda			you are too bold	K
Dipsacus, see Teasel				
Dipteracanthus Spectablis			fortitude	K
Dittany			childbirth	Du, Le
Dittany of Crete	Dittany	*Origanum dictamnus* (T)	birth	G, Ho, K, L, N, O, T
Dittany of Crete, White			passion	G, K, N
Dock	Patience	*Rumex patientia* (T)	patience	Du, G, Ho, K, L, Le, N,
				O, T
Dodder	Cuscuta, Dodder of Thyme	*Cuscuta epilimum* (Da),	baseness, meanness	Da, Du, G, K, L, Le, N,
				O, T
Dodder of Thyme			business	N
Dodder of Thyme			care	N
Dodder of Thyme			selfishness	N
Dodecatheon, see Cowslip				
Dog Rose, see Rose				
Dogsbane	Apocynum, Indian Hemp	*Apocynum andro-*	deceit, falsehood	Da, G, Ha, Ho, K, N,
		saemifolium (Da)		O
		Hypericifolium (Ha)		
Dogwood	Cornel Cherry/Tree,	*Cornus saguinea* (T)	durability, duration	G, Ho, K, L, Le, N,
	Wild Dogwood			O, T
Dogwood		*Cornus florida* (Da)	honesty	Da
Dogwood		*Cornus florida* (Wa)	love undiminished by	Wa
			adversity	
Dogwood		*Cornus florida* (Da)	true nobility	Da

FLOWER	OTHER COMMON NAME	BOTANICAL NAME	SENTIMENT	SOURCE
Dogwood Blossom			am I perfectly indifferent to you?	N
Double China Aster, see Aster				
Double Daisy or Marguerite, see Daisy				
Double Indian Pink, see Pink				
Double Larkspur, see Larkspur				
Double Red Carnation, see Pink				
Double Red Pink, see Pink				
Dracontium, see Arum				
Dragon Plant			snare	G, Ho, K, L, N, O
Dragon's Claw		*Corallorhiza adontorhiza* (Da)	danger	Da
Dragonwort			horror	G, K, N
Dried Flax, see Flax				
Dried White Rose, see Rose				
Dutchman's Pipe	Aristolochia	*Aristolochi sipha* (Da)	prodigality	Da
Dwarf Box, see Box				
Dwarf Pink		*Houstonia caerulea* (Da)	innocence	Da
Dwarf Sunflower, see Sunflower				
Dyer's Broom	Broom, Furze	*Genista* (E, P, Wa)	neatness	E, G, Ho, K, L, N, P, Wa
Dyer's Weed		*Reseda luteola* (Da)	design	Da
Ebenaster	Ebony	*Diospyros* (Da)	night	Da
Ebony			hypocrisy	O
Ebony			you are hard	N
Ebony Tree	Ebony		blackness	Du, G, Ho, K, L, Le, N, T
Echites Atropurpurea			be warned in time	K
Eglantine	Sweetbriar	*R. rubignosa* (Ha)	I wound to heal	Ha
Eglantine	Sweetbriar	*Rosa* (E), *R. rubignosa* (P, T, Wa)	poetry	A, Du, E, G, Ho, K, L, Le, N, P, T, Wa.
Eglantine, American	American Sweetbriar, Rose	*Rosa suavelens* (Wa)	imagination	Wa
Eglantine, American	American Sweetbriar, Rose	*Rosa suavelens* (M)	poetry	M, O
Eglantine, American	American Sweetbriar, Rose	*Rosa suavelens* (Ha)	simplicity	G, Ha, K, N, O
Elder		*Sambucus* (E), *S. niger* (Ha, P)	compassion	E, Ha, N, P
Elder		*Sambucus canadensis* (Da)	zeal, zealousness	Da, G, Ho, K, N, O
Eleagnus, see Oleaster				
Elm		*Ulmus* (Wa)	dignity	G, Ho, K, N, O, Wa
Elm, American		*Ulmus americana* (Da, Wa)	patriotism	Da, G, Ho, K, Wa
Elm, Yoke			ornament	T
Enchanter's Nightshade		*Circaea, C. lutetiana* (Wa)	fascination	O, Wa
Enchanter's Nightshade		*Circaea lutetiana* (Da, T)	sorcery, witchcraft	Da, G, Ho, K, O, T
Enchanter's Nightshade	Circae, Circee		spell	Du, G, K, L, Le
Endive			frugality	G, Ho, K, N, O
Endive		*Cichorium endivia* (Da)	medicine	Da
English Clematis, see Clematis				
English Moss, see Moss				
Entoca		*Entoca viscida* (Da)	gift, a gift	Da
Epigea, see Trailing Arbutus				
Epilobium, see Willow				
Erica, see Heather				
Escallonia		*Escallonia rubra* (Da)	opinion	Da
Eschscholzia			do not refuse me	K
Eternal Flower		*Xeranthemum annuum* (Da)	eternity	Da
Euonymus, see Spindle Tree				

169

FLOWER	OTHER COMMON NAME	BOTANICAL NAME	SENTIMENT	SOURCE
Eupatorium		*Eupatorium elegans* (Da)	delay	A, Da, G, Ho, K, N, O
Euphorbia		*Euphorbia splendens* (Da)	reproof	Da
Euphorbia Hypericifolia, see Eyebright				
Evening Primrose		*Oenothera odorata* (E)	I am more faithful than thou	E
Evening Primrose	Large-flowered	*Oenothera* (Wa), *O. biennis*	inconstancy	A, Du, G, Ha, Ho, K,
	Evening Primrose	(T), *O. odorata* (Ha, M, P)		L, Le, M, N, O, P,
				T, Wa
Evening Primrose		*Oenothera odorata* (P)	silent love	K, P
Evening Primrose				
Everblooming Candytuft, see Candytuft				
Evergreen			poverty	O
Evergreen	Wintergreen	*Chirraphila, Gaultheria,*	poverty and worth	A, E, Ho
		Pyrola (E)		
Evergreen Clematis, see Clematis				
Evergreen Thorn, Everlasting Thorn	Firethorn	*Mespilus pyracantha* (Wa)	solace in adversity	G, Ho, K, Wa
Everlasting		*Gnaphalium* (E, Ha, M, P)	always remembered,	E, G, Ha, Ho, K, M,
				O, P
Everlasting Pea, see Pea				
Eyebright		*Euphorbia hypericifolia* (Da)	your eyes are bewitching	Da
Fagus, see Beech				
Fair Maids of France, see Buttercup				
False Dragon Head	Lion's Heart	*Physostegia virginiana* (Da)	bravery	Da
False Narcissus, see Daffodil, Narcissus				
False White Cedar, see Arbor Vitae				
Feathery Reed, see Reed				
Fennel		*Anethum* (M, Wa),	force, strength	Du, G, K, L, Le, M, N,
		A. foeniculum (T)		O, T, Wa
Fennel		*Anethum graveolens* (Da)	worthy all praise	Da, G, Ho, K
Fennel Flower, see Love-in-a-Mist				
Fern			fascination	G, Ho, K
Fern			magic	G, K
Fern		*Filicia* (Wa)	sincerity	G, K, L, N, O, T, Wa
Fern, Flowering		*Osmunda regalis* (T)	reverie	G, K, N, O, T
Fern, Maidenhair		*Adiantum capillus-veneris* (T)	discretion	L, N, O, T
Fern, Maidenhair			secrecy	Du, Le, O
Fern, Royal		*Osmunda regalis* (Da)	dreams, reverie	A, G, K, L
Fern, Walking		*Antigramma rhizophylla* (Da)	curiosity	Da
Feverfew		*Matricaria parthenoides* (Da)	beneficence	Da
Ficoides, see Ice Plant				
Field Anemone, see Anemone				
Field Bindweed, see Convolvulus				
Fig			argument	G, Ho, K, N, O
Fig			longevity	Du, L, N
Fig Marigold, see Dew Plant, Mesembryanthemum				
Fig Tree			prolific, profuseness	G, Ho, K, N, O
Filbert, see Hazel				
Filicia, see Fern				
Fir of Gilead			juice	N
Fir, see Pine				
Firethorn, see Evergreen Thorn				
Fish Geranium, see Geranium				
Flame Iris, see Iris				

171

FLOWER	OTHER COMMON NAME	BOTANICAL NAME	SENTIMENT	SOURCE
Fuller's Teasel, see Teasel				
Fumitory		*Fumaria officinalis* (T)	hatred	T
Fumitory	Common Fumitory		gall, spleen	G, Ho, K, L, N, O
Furze, see Broom, Gorse				
Galanthus, see Snowdrop				
Galega, see Goat's Rue				
Galium, see Bed Straw				
Garden Anemone, see Anemone				
Garden Chervil, see Chervil				
Garden Daisy, see Daisy				
Garden Marigold, see Marigold				
Garden Ranunculus, see Buttercup				
Garden Sage, see Sage				
Garden Stock, see Wallflower				
Gardenia			refinement	K
Garland of Roses, see Roses				
Gathered Flowers			we die together	T
Gelsemium, see Jasmine				
Genista, see Broom, Dyer's Broom				
Gentian			I love you best when you are sad	K
Gentian		*Gentiana acaulis* (Da)	intrinsic worth	Da
Gentian		*Gentiana* (E, P), *Gentiana fritillaria* (O)	virgin pride	E, O, P
Gentian, Yellow			ingratitude	Ho, O
Gentle Balm, see Balm				
Geranium		*Geranium sanguineum* (Da)	confidence	Da
Geranium		*Pelargonium capitatum* (P)	deceit	K, P
Geranium		*Pelargonium* (Ha, Wa)	gentility	Ha, N, Wa
Geranium, Apple			present preference	N
Geranium, Dark			melancholy	G, K, N
Geranium, Fish			disappointed expectation	N
Geranium, Ivy		*Pelargonium peltatum* (Ha)	bridal favor	G, K, Ha
Geranium, Ivy			I engage you for the next dance	N
Geranium, Lemon		*Pelargonium acerifolium* (E, Ha, M)	serenity, tranquility of mind	E, Ha, M
Geranium, Lemon			unexpected meeting	G, K
Geranium, Mourning		*Pelargonium triste* (Ha)	despondency	A, Ha
Geranium, Nutmeg		*Pelargonium odoratissimum* (Ha)	expected meeting	Ha, G, K, N
Geranium, Oak			lady, deign to smile	N
Geranium, Oak	Oak-leaved Geranium	*Pelargonium quercifolium* (E, Ha, M)	true friendship	E, G, Ha, K, M
Geranium, Penciled-leaf			ingenuity	Du, G, K, Le, N
Geranium, Rose-scented		*Pelargonium capitatum* (E, Ha, M, P, T)	preference	Du, E, G, Ha, K, L, Le, M, N, O, P, T
Geranium, Scarlet		*Pelargonium inquinans* (Ha)	consolation, comforting	G, Ha, K, N
Geranium, Scarlet	Horseshoe-leaf Geranium		folly, stupidity	Du, K, L, Le, N, T
Geranium, Scarlet			preference	Ho
Geranium, Scarlet		*Pelargonium inquinans* (E, M)	thou art changed	E, M
Geranium, Silver-leaved		*Pelargonium argentifolium* (E, Ha, M, P)	recall	E, G, Ha, K, M, N, P
Geranium, Sorrowful	Night-smelling Geranium	*Pelargonium triste* (T)	melancholy mind/spirit	Du, L, Le, N, O, T
Geranium, Wild			steadfast piety	Du, G, K, Le
German Iris, see Iris				

FLOWER	OTHER COMMON NAME	BOTANICAL NAME	SENTIMENT	SOURCE
Germander Speedwell, see Speedwell				
Gilia, see Ipomopsis				
Gillyflower			dignity	L
Gillyflower, see also Wallflower				
Gladiolus		*Gladiolus communis* (Da)	ready armed	Da, K
Gladiolus		*Gladiolus communis* (Da)	strength of character	Da, K
Glasswort			pretension	
Globe Amaranth		*Gomphrena* (E)	hope in misery	E
Globe Amaranth		*Gomphrena globosa* (Da, Ha, M)	I change not, unchangeable	Da, Ha, M, N
Globe Amaranth		*Gomphrena perennis* (Da)	immortality	Da, G, K, L
Globe-flowered Fuchsia, see Fuchsia				
Glory Flower	Clianthus, Crimson Glory Flower	*Clianthus dampieri* (Da) *Clianthus puniceus* (Wa)	glorious beauty	Da, G, Ho, K, O, Wa
Glycine		*Glycine sinensis* (T)	your friendship is pleasing and agreeable to me	T
Gnaphalium, see Everlasting				
Goat's Rue	Galega	*Galega officinalis* (T)	reason	G, Ho, K, L, N, O, T
Golden Bartonia, see Bartonia				
Golden Locks, Flax-leaved			tardiness	G, Ho, K, O
Golden Rod		*Solidago* (E), *S. speciosa* (Ha, P)	encouragement	E, Ha, N, P
Golden Rod		*Solidago virgaurea* (Da)	precaution	Da, G, Ho, K, N, O
Gomphrena, see Globe Amaranth				
Good King Henry, see Goosefoot				
Gooseberry			anticipation	G, K, N
Goosefoot	Bonus Henricus, Good King Henry	*Chenopodium* (Wa), *C. bonus henricus* (T)	goodness, kindness	G, Ho, K, L, N, O, T, Wa
Goosefoot				
Goosefoot, Grass-leaved		*Chenopodium altissimum* (T)	I declare war against you	T
Gorse	Furze, Whin	*Ulex europaeus* (Wa)	cheerfulness in adversity	Ho, O, Wa
Gorse	Furze, Whin		enduring affection	N
Gorse, see Broom				
Gossypium, see Cotton Plant				
Gourd	Pumpkin	*Cucurbita pepo* (T), *Lagenaria vulgaris* (Da)	bulkiness, extent, plumpness	Da, G, K, L, N, T
Gramen, see Grass				
Grammanthus Chloraflora			your temper is too hasty	G, K
Grape	Wild Grape	*Vitis* (E)	charity	E, Ho, O
Grape, Wild		*Vitis vinifera* (Ha, M)	mirth	Ha, M
Grass		*Gramina* (E, Ha, P)	submission	E, G, Ha, Ho, K, N, P
Grass		*Anthoxanthum odoratum* (Da), *Gramen* (Wa)	usefulness, utility	Da, Du, G, K, L, Le, N, O, T, Wa
Grass, Canary		*Phalaris canariensis* (Da)	perseverance	Da, G, Ho, K, N, O
Grass, Foxtail			sporting	G, K
Grass, Trembling		*Briza media* (T)	frivolity	T
Grass, Vernal		*Anthoxanthum* (E, Ha)	poor but happy	E, G, Ha, Ho, K, N, O
Great Bindweed, see Convolvulus				
Greek Valerian, see Valerian				
Green-leaved Locust Tree, see Locust				
Ground Cherry, see Winter Cherry				
Ground Ivy		*Nepeta glechoma* (Da)	enjoyment	Da
Ground Laurel, see Laurel				
Ground Pine		*Lycopodium complanatum* (Da)	complaint	Da
Groundsel Tree	Baccharis	*Baccharis halimifolia* (Da)	intoxication	Da

173

FLOWER	OTHER COMMON NAME	BOTANICAL NAME	SENTIMENT	SOURCE
Guelder Rose, see Snowball				
Gum Cistus, see Cistus				
Gum Tree		*Nyssa multiflora* (Da)	enthusiasm	Da
Hackmetack	Larch, Tamarack		single blessedness	A
Halesia, see Snowdrop Tree				
Hamamelis, see Witch Hazel				
Hand Flower Tree			warning	G, K
Harebell, see Bellflower				
Hawkweed		*Hieracium gronovii* (Da)	quick-sightedness	Da, G, Ho, K, O
Hawthorn		*Crataegus* (E, Ha, P, Wa),	hope	A, Du, E, G, Ha, Ho,
		C. oxyacantha (T)		K, L, Le, P, O, T, Wa
Hazel		*Corylus avellana* (T)	peace	Du, Le, T
Hazel	Filbert	*Corylus* (E, P),	reconciliation	Du, E, G, Ho, K, L,
		C. avellana (T, Wa)		Le, N, O, P, T, Wa
Heartsease, see Pansy				
Heath, see Heather				
Heather	Heath	*Erica* (M, Wa),	solitude, solitude is	A, Da, G, Ho, K, L, Le,
		E. odorata (Da, T)	sometimes the best society	M, O, P, T, W
Heather, White			good luck	T
Hedera, see Ivy				
Hedysarum, see Sainfoin				
Helenium		*Helenium autumnale* (Da, T)	tears	A, Da, Du, G, Ho, K, L,
				Le, O, T
Helianthus, see Sunflower				
Heliotrope	Peruvian Heliotrope	*Heliotropium* (E, Ha, M, P),	devotion, devoted attachment	Da, E, G, Ha, K, Le, M,
		H. peruvianum (Da)		P
Heliotrope			faithfulness	G
Heliotrope	Peruvian Heliotrope		I trust in thee	O
Heliotrope			I turn to thee	K
Heliotrope	Peruvian Heliotrope	*Heliotropium* (Wa),	infatuation, I love you	Ho, L, Wa, T
		H. peruvianum (T)		
Heliotrope	Peruvian Heliotrope	*Heliotropium* (Wa),	intoxication,	Ho, L, Wa
			intoxicated with pleasure	
Hellebore		*Helleborus viridis* (Da),	calumny	Da, G, Ha, Ho, K, O
		H. niger (Ha)		
Hellebore			scandal	G, K
Helmet Flower, see Monkshood				
Hemerocallis, see Day Lily				
Hemlock			you will be/cause my death	G, Ho, K, O
Hemp		*Cannabis sativa* (Da)	fate	Da, G, K
Henbane		*Hysocyamus niger* (T)	defect, fault, imperfection	G, Ho, K, L, O, T
Hepatica	Liverwort	*Hepatica triloba* (T)	confidence, trust	Du, G, K, L, Le, N, O, T
Herb Willow, see Willow				
Hesperis, see Rocket				
Hibiscus		*Hibiscus* (E)	beauty is vain	E
Hibiscus	Flower of an Hour, Venetian Mallow	*Hibiscus* (P), *H. trionum* (Ha)	delicate beauty	G, Ha, Ho, K, N, O, P
Hibiscus	Flower of an Hour	*Hisbiscus trionum* (Da)	trifling beauty	Da
Hibiscus, see also Mallow				
Hickory		*Carya alba* (Wa)	glory	Ho, O, Wa
Hieracium, see Hawkweed				
Hippomane, see Manchineel				
Hoarhound			frozen kindness	Ho, O

174

FLOWER	OTHER COMMON NAME	BOTANICAL NAME	SENTIMENT	SOURCE
Hoarhound, Black		*Ballota nigra* (Da)	I reject you	Da
Holly		*Ilex* (Ha, M, P)	domestic happiness	Ha, M, P
Holly		*Ilex* (Wa), *I. aquifolium* (Da, T)	foresight	Da, Du, G, Ho, K, L, Le, O, T, Wa
Holly Herb, see Vervain				
Hollyhock		*Althea* (E), *Althea rosea* (Da, Ha, M, P)	ambition	Da, Du, E, G, Ha, K, Le, M, P
Hollyhock	Rose Mallow	*Althea rosea* (T, Wa)	fruitfulness, fecundity	G, Ho, K, L, O, T, Wa
Honesty		*Lunaria annua* (Ha)	fascination	G, Ha, K
Honesty	Lunaria, Moonwort, Satin Flower	*Lunaria biennis* (T)	forgetfulness	A, Du, G, K, L, Le, N, O, T
Honesty	Satin Flower	*Lunaria* (Wa), *L. biennis* (Da)	honesty	Da, G, Ho, K, O, Wa
Honey Flower		*Melianthus* (Ha, M, P)	love sweet and secret, my love is sweet and secret	G, Ha, K, M, P
Honeysuckle	Woodbine	*Caprifolium periclymenum* (T), *Lonicera* (Wa), *L. periclymenum* (Da)	bonds of love	Da, Ho, L, O, Wa
Honeysuckle		*Lonicera sempervirens* (P)	devoted love, generous and devoted affection	Du, G, K, Le, P
Honeysuckle	Coral Honeysuckle	*Lonicera* (E), *L. sempervirens* (Ha, P)	fidelity	E, Ha, P
Honeysuckle	Woodbine	*Lonicera* (E), *L. periclymenun* (Ha, M, P)	fraternal love	A, E, G, Ha, K, M, P
Honeysuckle, Coral	Coral Honeysuckle		the color of my fate	G, K
Honeysuckle, French	French Honeysuckle		rustic beauty	G, Ho, K, O
Honeysuckle, Trumpet	Trumpet Honeysuckle		I have dreamed of thee	A
Honeysuckle, Wild	Wild Honeysuckle	*Azalea procumbens* (Ha)	inconstancy	Ha
Hops		*Humulus* (E, Wa), *H. lupulus* (Da)	injustice	Da, Du, E, G, Ho, K, L, Le, O, T, Wa
Hornbeam, Hornbeam Tree			ornament	Du, G, Ho, K, L, Le, O
Horse Chestnut	Buckeye	*Aesculus hippocastanum* (Da, T, Wa)	luxury, luxuriancy	Da, G, Ho, K, Le, O, T, Wa
Horseshoe-leaf Geranium, see Geranium				
Houseleek			domestic industry	G, K
Houseleek		*Sempervivum tectorum* (Da, Wa)	vivacity	Da, G, K, Wa
Houstonia	Bluet, Quaker-Ladies	*Houstonia* (Ha), *H. cerulea* (E, M, P)	content, contentment, quiet happiness	A, E, G, Ha, Ho, K, M, P, O
Houstonia, see Dwarf Pink				
Hoya		*Hoya carnosa* (Da)	sculpture	Da, G, Ho, K, O
Hoyabella			contentment	K
Humbleplant			despondency	G, K
Humulus, see Hops				
Hundred-leaved Rose, see Rose				
Hyacinth			benevolence	L
Hyacinth			come, play	Du
Hyacinth	Blue Hyacinth	*Hyacinthus* (Ha), *H. comosus* (Ho)	constancy	Ha, Ho, P
Hyacinth		*Hyacinthus comosus* (P), *H. orientalis*	game	G, Ho, K, L, Le, P, T
Hyacinth	Purple Hyacinth	*Hyacinthus comosus* (Ha, P)	grief, sorrow, sorrowful, I am sorry	A, Ha, K, P, O
Hyacinth		*Hyacinthus orientalis* (Da)	jealousy	Da
Hyacinth			sport	G, K, L

175

FLOWER	OTHER COMMON NAME	BOTANICAL NAME	SENTIMENT	SOURCE
Hyacinth		*Hyacinthus* (Wa),	play	Du, P, Ho, G, K, L,
		H. orientalis (T)		Le, T, Wa
Hyacinth, White			unobtrusive loveliness	G, K
Hyacinth, Wild	Bluebell	*Scilla nonscripta* (T)	kindness	T
Hydrangea	Hydranger	*Hydrangea hortensis* (Wa)	boaster	Da, G, Ho, K, O, Wa
Hydrangea		*Hydrangea* (E),	heartlessness	A, E, G, Ha, P
		H. hortensis (Ha, P)		
Hydrangea	Hortensia	*Hydrangea hortensis* (T)	you are cold	Du, G, K, L, Le, O, T
Hypericum, see Saint John's Wort				
Hysocyamus, see Henbane				
Hyssop			cleanliness	G, K
Hyssop		*Hyssop officinalis* (Da)	purification	Da
Iberis, see Candytuft				
Ice Plant		*Mesembryanthemum*	an old beau	Ha
		crystallinum (Ha)		
Ice Plant		*Mesembryanthemum*	formality	Da
		crystallinum (Da)		
Ice Plant	Ficoides	*Mesembryanthemum* (E),	your looks freeze me,	Du, E, G, Ho, K, L,
		M. crystallinum (T, Wa)	you freeze me	Le, O, T, Wa
Ice Moss, Iceland Moss, see Moss				
Ilex, see Holly				
Imbricata			uprightness, sentiments of	E
			honor	
Impatiens, see Balsam				
Imperial Montague, see Crown Imperial				
Indian Corn, see Corn				
Indian Cress	Sweet Sedge, Three-	*Tropeolum tricolorum* (Wa)	resignation	A, G, K, Ho, O, Wa
	Colored Indian Cress			
Indian Cress			warlike trophy	G, K
Indian Fig, see Cactus				
Indian Hemp, see Dogsbane				
Indian Jasmine		*Bignonia radicans* (T)	separation	T
Indian Jasmine, see also Ipomoea				
Indian Mallow		*Abutilon avicennae* (Da)	estimation	Da
Indian Plum, see Myrobalan				
Ipomoea, see also Morning Glory	Quamoclit	*Ipomoea* (Wa)	busybody	G, Ho, K, N, O, Wa
Ipomoea	Cypress Vine, Indian Jas-	*Ipomoea coccinea* (T, Wa)	attachment,	Da, Du, G, Ho, K,
	mine, Quamoclit, Red	*Quamoclit vulgaris* (Da)	I attach myself to you	Le, N,O, T, Wa
	Jasmine of India, Scarlet			
	Ipomoea			
Ipomopsis	Standing Cypress	*Gilia coronopifolia* (Da)	suspense	Da
Iris	Crested Iris, Fleur de Lis,		fire, I burn	G, K
Iris	Fleur de Luce, Flower	*Iris* (E, Wa), *I. cristata* (M, P),	message	Da, Du, E, G, Ho, K,
	de Luce	*I. sambucina* (Da)		L, Le, M, O, P, T,
				Wa
Iris	Crested Iris, Flower de	*Iris cristata* (Ha)	my compliments	Ha
	Luce			
Iris, Flame, German, or Yellow	Fleur de Lis, Flower	*Iris germanica* (T)	flame	Du, G, Ho, K, L, Le,
	de Luce			N, T
Iris, German		*Iris germanica* (T)	ardor	T
Iris, Yellow			passion, flame of love, passion	Ho, N, O
Ivy			fidelity	G, Ho, K, N

FLOWER	OTHER COMMON NAME	BOTANICAL NAME	SENTIMENT	SOURCE
Lake Flower		*Limnanthemum lacunosa* (Da)	retirement	Da
Lancaster Rose, see Rose				
Lantana		*Lantana mexicana* (Da)	rigor	Da, G, Ho, K, L, N, O
Lantana		*Lantana camara* (T)	sharpness	T
Lapageria Rosea			there is no unalloyed good	K
Lappa Major, see Burdock				
Larch			audacity	G, K, L, N
Larch		*Larix communis* (T)	boldness	Du, G, K, Le, N, O, T
Larix, see Larch				
Larkspur		*Delphinium ajacis* (Wa)	ardent attachment	Wa
Larkspur	Pink Larkspur, Single Larkspur	*Delphinium* (E, Ha, P), *D. consolidum* (M)	fickleness, inconstancy	A, E, G, Ha, K, M, N, P
Larkspur	Double Larkspur, Purple Larkspur	*Delphinium* (Ha)	haughtiness	G, Ha, K
Larkspur		*Delphinium grandiflorum* (Da)	levity, lightness	Da, Du, G, Ho, K, L, Le, N, O
Larkspur		*Delphinium consolida* (T)	swiftness	T
Lathrea, see Toothwort				
Lathyrus, see Pea				
Laurel	Bay, Bay Wreath, Red Bay, Sweet Bay	*Laurus caroliniana* (Ha), *L. nobilis* (Da, T), *Prunus laurocerasus* (Wa)	glory	Da, Du, G, Ha, Ho, K, L, Le, N, O, T, Wa
Laurel	Bay Leaf, Bay Tree	*Laurus* (E, Ha, M, P)	I change but in dying	A, E, G, Ha, Ho, K, M, P
Laurel	Red Bay	*Laurus caroliniana* (Wa)	love's memory, love and memory	Ho, N, O, Wa
Laurel	Bay, Bay Wreath, Red Bay, Sweet Bay	*Laurus nobilis* (Wa)	reward of merit	G, Ho, K, Wa
Laurel	Sweet Bay	*Laurus nobilis* (T)	treachery	T
Laurel	American Laurel	*Klamia* (E, Ha)	virtue is true beauty, virtue makes her charming	E, Ha
Laurel				
Laurel, Common in Flower	Almond Laurel, Cherry Laurel		perfidity	G, Ho, K, L, N, O
Laurel, Ground			perseverance	G, K
Laurel, Mountain		*Rhododendron* (Ha, P, Wa)	ambition	G, Ha, K, N, P, Wa
Laurel-leaved Magnolia, see Magnolia				
Laurestina, Laurustinus		*Viburnum tinus* (Ha, Wa)	token, a token	G, Ha, K, N
Laurestine, Laurustinus		*Viburnum tinus* (Da, M, T, Wa)	I die if neglected	Da, Du, G, Ho, L, Le, M, N, O, T, Wa
Laurus, see Laurel				
Lavatera see Mallow				
Lavender		*Lavandula* (E), *L. spica* (Ha, M)	acknowledgement	E, Ha, M
Lavender			assiduity	Ho, O
Lavender		*Lavandula spica* (Da)	confession	Da
Lavender		*Lavandula spica* (Da, T)	mistrust, distrust	Du, G, K, L, Le, N, T
Lavender, Sea, see Sea Lavender			dauntlessness	N
Leaf, Leaves	Dead Leaves		sadness, sorrow	A, Du, G, K, L, Le, N, O, T
Leaf, Walking			how came you here?	O
Leaves, Autumnal	Dead Leaves		melancholy	Du, G, K, L, Le, P, T
Lemon		*Citrus limonia* (P)	zest	G, Ho, K, N, O, P
Lemon Balm, see Balm				
Lemon Blossom			fidelity in love	G, K, N
Lemon Geranium, see Geranium				

FLOWER	OTHER COMMON NAME	BOTANICAL NAME	SENTIMENT	SOURCE
Lemon, Lemon Blossom		*Citrus* (E), *Citrus limonia* (Da, Ha, P)	discretion	Da, E, Ha, N, P
Leontodon, see Dandelion				
Leschenaultia Splendens			you are charming	K
Lesser Celandine, see Celandine				
Lettuce		*Lactuca* (P), *L. sativa* (Da, T)	cold hearted, coldness	A, Da, E, G, Ho, K, N, O, P, T
Lettuce			cooling down	L
Liana			knot, alliance	L
Lichen	Tall Moss	*Usrea* (P	dejection	G, K, N, P
Lichen	Tall Moss	*Usrea* (Ha, P)	solitude	G, Ha, Ho, K, N, O, P
Licorice, Wild			I declare against you	G, K, N
Ligustrum, see Privet				
Lilac	Persian Lilac, Purple Lilac	*Syringa* (E, P, Wa), *S. persica* (Da), *S. vulgaris* (T)	first emotion of love, awakening love	A, Da, Du, E, G, K, L, Le, N, O, P, T, Wa
Lilac			forsaken	Ho
Lilac			fastidiousness	Ha, P
Lilac, Field	Purple Lilac	*Syringa* (Ha, P)	humility	G, K, N
Lilac, Field			joy of worth	G, K
Lilac, White			modesty, purity	N
Lilac, White		*Syringa vulgaris* (Ha)	youth, youthful innocence	Du, G, Ha, L, Le, N, O, T
Lilac Polyanthus, see Auricula				
Lilies			you cannot deceive me	K
Lilies, Japanese			majesty	Du, L, Le, P, T
Lily	White Lily	*Lilium candidum* (P, T)	purity	A, Da, E
Lily	White Lily	*Lilium candidum* (Da, E)	purity and beauty	Ha
Lily	White Lily	*Lilium candidum* (Ha)	purity and modesty	G, Ho, K, O, Wa
Lily	White Lily	*Lilium candidum* (Wa)	purity and sweetness	G, K, M, N, P
Lily	White Lily	*Lilium candidum* (M, P)	delicate simplicity	Ha, M, P
Lily of the Valley		*Convallaria majalis* (Ha, M, P)		
Lily of the Valley		*Convallaria* (E)	the heart withering in secret	E
Lily of the Valley		*Convallaria majalis* (Da, P, T, Wa)	return of happiness	Da, Du, G, Ho, K, L, Le, N, O, P, T, Wa
Lily of the Valley			unconscious sweetness	K
Lily of the Valley		*Lilium carolinianum* (Ha)	high-souled	Ha
Lily, Scarlet		*Lilium superbum* (Wa)	splendor	Wa
Lily, Superb			coquetry	Wa
Lily, Yellow			falsehood	G, K, N
Lily, Yellow		*Lilium luteum* (Ha)	gaiety, playful gaiety	G, Ha, K, N
Lily, Yellow				
Limnanthemum, see Lake Flower				
Linden or Lime Tree		*Tilia* (Wa), *T. rubra* (T)	conjugal fidelity/love	Du, G, Ho, K, L, Le, N, O, T, Wa
Linden, American	Bass-wood	*Tilia americana* (Da, Wa)	matrimony	A, Da, G, Ho, K, Wa
Lint			I feel my obligations	G, K, N
Linum, see Flax				
Lion's Heart, see False Dragon Head				
Liriodendron, see Tulip Tree				
Live Oak, see Oak				
Liverwort, see Hepatica				
Loasa		*Loasa lateritia* (Da)	pleasure	Da
Lobelia		*Lobelia fulgens* (Wa)	arrogance	Ho, Wa

FLOWER	OTHER COMMON NAME	BOTANICAL NAME	SENTIMENT	SOURCE
Lobelia		*Lobelia fulgens* (Da),	malevolence	Da, G, Ha, K, N
		L. cardinalis (Ha)		
Lobelia			splendor	O
Lobelia, see Cardinal Flower				
Locust	Green-leaved Locust Tree	*Robinia* (E), *R. caragana* (Ha,	affection beyond the grave	A, E, G, Ha2, K, M,
		P), *R. pseudo-acacia* (M)		N, P
Locust		*Robinia pseudacacia* (Da, Wa)	vicissitude	Da, Ho, O, Wa
Locust Tree			elegance	G, K, N
Lolium, see Darnel				
London Pride		*Saxifraga umbrosa* (Wa),	frivolity	Du, E, G, Ho, K, Le,
		Silene (E, M, P)		M, N, O, P, Wa
Lonicera, see Honeysuckle				
Lophospermum	Maurandia	*Lophospermum scandens* (Da)	ecstasy	Da
Lote Tree			concord	G, K
Lotos, Lotus, see Clover, Water Lily				
Love in a Puzzle			embarrassment	Ho, N, O
Love-in-a-Mist	Fennel Flower	*Nigella damascena* (Da)	artifice	Da
Love-in-a-Mist	Fennel Flower	*Nigella damascena* (A, M)	you puzzle me, perplexity	A, G, Ho, K, M, N, O
Love-Lies-Bleeding	Love-Lies-A-Bleeding	*Amaranthus caudatus* (P),	hopeless, not heartless	G, Ha, Ho, K, M, N,
		A. hypocondriacus (Ha, M)		O, P
Lucern	Alfalfa, Medick	*Medicago sativa* (Da)	agriculture	Da
Lucern	Alfalfa, Medick	*Medicago sativa* (T, Wa)	life	A, Du, G, Ho, K, L,
				Le, N, O, T, Wa
Lunaria, see Honesty				
Lupine		*Lupinus* (E, Ha), *L. hirsutus*	dejection, sorrow	E, Ha, M
		(M)		
Lupine			imagination	G
Lupine		*Lupinus polyphyllus* (Da)	voraciousness	Da, G, Ho, K, N, O
Lychnis	Bachelor's Button	*Lychnis dioica* (M)	ever till now	M
Lychnis	Bachelor's Button	*Lychnis dioica* (Ha)	hope in love	Ha
Lychnis			a religious enthusiast,	Ho, N, O
			religious enthusiasm	
Lychnis, Meadow	Ragged Robin	*Lychnis flos-cuculi* (Da)	wit	Da, G, Ho, K, N, O
Lychnis, Scarlet			sun-beamed eyes	G, K, N
Lycopodium, see Ground Pine				
Lythrum, see Willow				
Madder		*Rubia tinctorum* (T)	calumny, slander	Du, G, Ho, K, L, Le,
				N, O, T
Madwort, Rock		*Alyssum saxatile* (T),	tranquility	Ho, O, T, Wa
		Asperugo (Wa)		
Magnolia		*Magnolia grandiflora* (Da),	love of nature	Da, G, Ha, K, N, P
		M. glauca (Ha, P)		
Magnolia		*Magnolia glauca* (P)	magnificence	K, P
Magnolia			peerless and proud	O
Magnolia, Laurel-leaved		*Magnolia grandiflora*	high-souled	Wa
Magnolia, Laurel-leaved			dignity	G, Ho, K
Magnolia, Swamp			perseverance	G, K, N
Mahon's Stock, see Stock				
Maiden-blush Rose, see Rose				
Maidenhair Fern, see Fern				
Maidwort			tranquility	N
Maize, see Corn				
Mallow		*Malva sylvestris* (Da)	goodness	Da
Mallow			mild or sweet disposition	O

180

FLOWER	OTHER COMMON NAME	BOTANICAL NAME	SENTIMENT	SOURCE
Mallow			mildness	G, K
Mallow, Marsh			humanity	Ho, O
Mallow, Marsh		*Althea officinalis* (T)	beneficence	Du, G, K, L, Le, N, T
Mallow, Marsh		*Lavatera* (E, P)	sweet disposition	E, Ho, P.
Mallow, Syrian		*Althea frutex* (M),	consumed by love	G, Ha, K, M, N
		Hibiscus syriacus (Ha)		
Mallow, Syrian	Althea Frutex		persuasion	G, K, Ho, N, O.
Malon Creeana			will you share my fortunes?	K
Malva sylvestris, see Mallow				
Manchineel Tree			falsehood	Du, G, K, L, Le, N, O
Manchineel Tree			hypocrisy	N
Manchineel		*Hippomane mancinella* (T)	duplicity	L, T
Mandrake			horror	G, K, N
Mandrake		*Mandragora officinalis* (T)	rarity	Du, Ho, L, Le, O, T .
Manrandia, see Maurandia				
Maple		*Acer* (E, P),	reserve	E, G, Ho, K, L, Le,
		A. campestre (Wa)		N, O, P, Wa
Maple		*Acer campestre* (Wa)	retirement	Wa
Maple, Rock		*Acer saccharinum* (Da)	rescue	Da
Marguerite, see Daisy				
Marianthus			hope for better days	G, K
Marigold	Calendula	*Calendula* (E),	contempt	E, P
		C. officinalis (P)		
Marigold		*Tagetes erecta* (Da)	cruelty	Da
Marigold		*Calendula officinalis* (P)	grief	Du, G, K, Le, N, P
Marigold		*Calendula* (Wa)	inquietude	O, Wa
Marigold and Cypress			despair	Du, G, Ho, K, L, Le,.
				N, T
Marigold and Cypress			melancholy	N
Marigold, African			vulgar minds, vulgar-minded	G, Ho, K, N, O
Marigold, French		*Tagetes patula* (Ha, M)	jealousy	A, G, Ha, Ho, K, M, .
				N, O
Marigold, Garden			uneasiness	G, Ho, K, O.
Marigold, Prophetic			prediction	Du, G, K, L
Marigold, Small Cape		*Calendula pluvialis* (T)	omen, presage	O, T
Marigold, Water			foreboding	L
Marigold, Yellow	Calendula, Garden Marigold, Yellow Marigold	*Calendula officinalis* (Ha)	sacred affections	A, Ha
Marjoram	Sweet Marjoram	*Origanum majorana* (Da)	blushes	Da, G, Ho, K, N, O...
Marsh Andromeda		*Andromeda hypnoides* (Da)	bound by fate	Da
Marsh Mallow, see Mallow				
Maruta cotula, see Mayweed				
Marvel of Peru, see Four-o'clock				
Matricaria, see Feverfew				
Matthiola, see Stock				
Maurandia	Manrandia	*Maurandia sempervirens* (Da)	courtesy	Da
Maurandia, see Lophospermum				
May Flower, see Trailing Arbutus				
May Rose, see Rose				
Mayweed		*Maruta cotula* (Da)	rumor	Da
Meadow Lychnis, see Lychnis				
Meadow Saffron	Autumn Crocus	*Colchicum autumnale* , (Da, Ha2), *C. officinalis* (M)	growing old, I do not fear to grow old	Da, E, Ha2, M
Meadow Saffron	Autumn Crocus	*Colchicum autumnale* (T), *C. officinalis* (A)	my best/happiest days are gone	A, Du, G, Ho, K, L,.. Le, N, O, T

FLOWER	OTHER COMMON NAME	BOTANICAL NAME	SENTIMENT	SOURCE
Meadowsweet	Queen of the Meadow, Spirae Hypericum Frutex	*Spiraea salicifolia* (Da)	praise	Da
Meadowsweet	Queen of the Meadow, Spirae Hypericum Frutex	*Spiraea ulmaria* (T, Wa)	uselessness	G, Ho, K, L, N, O, T, Wa
Medicago, Medick, see Lucern				
Melianthus, see Honey Flower				
Melilot	Sweet-scented Clover	*Melilotus alba* (Da)	philanthropy	Da
Melissa, see Balm				
Melon, see Watermelon				
Mentha, see Mint, Peppermint				
Mentzelia, see Bartonia				
Menyanthes, see Buckbean				
Mercury			goodness	G, Ho, K, O
Mermaid Weed		*Proserpinaca palustris* (Da)	necessity	Da
Mesembryanthemum	Fig Marigold		idleness	A, G, Ho, K, N, O
Mesembryanthemum, see Dew Plant, Ice Plant				
Mespilus, see Evergreen Thorn, Everlasting Thorn				
Mezereon, see Daphne				
Michaelmas Daisy, see Aster				
Mignonette		*Reseda odorata* (E)	moral and intellectual beauty	E
Mignonette		*Reseda odorata* (Da, Ha, M, P, T, Wa)	your qualities surpass your charms/loveliness	Da, Du, G, Ha, Ho, K, L, Le, M, N, O, P, T, Wa
Milfoil, Common, see Yarrow				
Milkvetch			your presence softens my pain	G, Ho, K, N, O
Milkweed		*Asclepias cornutii* (Da)	conquer your love	Da
Milkwort	Polygala	*Polygala vulgaris* (T)	hermitage	Du, L, Le, N, T
Mimosa	Sensitive Plant	*Mimosa* (E), *Mimosa sensitiva* (Ha, M)	sensibility, sensitiveness	E, G, Ha, Ho, K, M, N, O
Mimulus, see Musk Plant				
Mint		*Mentha viridis* (Da)	virtue	Da, G, Ho, K, N, O
Mirabilis, see Four-o'clock				
Mistletoe		*Viscum alba* (Wa)	parasite	Wa
Mistletoe		*Viscum alba* (T), *V. verticillatum* (M)	I rise above/surmount all difficulties/obstacles	Du, G, K, L, Le, M, N, O
Mistletoe		*Phoradendron flavescens* (Da)	obstacles to be overcome/ surmounted	Da, Ho
Mitraria Coccinea			dullness, indolence	G, K
Mock Orange			counterfeit	G, Ho, K, N
Mock Orange, see Syringa				
Moluccella, see Balm				
Momordica, see Cucumber				
Monarda	Balm, Mountain Mint, Wild Balm	*Monarda didyma* (Da)	I value your sympathy	Da
Monarda Amplexicaulis	Balm		your whims are quite unbearable	K
Monkshood			a deadly foe is near	K
Monkshood	Helmet Flower, Wolfsbane	*Aconitum napellus* (Da)	chivalry, knight errantry	Da, G, Ho, K, O
Monkshood	Helmet Flower, Wolfsbane	*Aconitum napellus* (Ha)	deceit	Ha
Monkshood	Helmet Flower, Wolfsbane		misanthropy	G, K, N
Monthly Rose, see Rose, China				
Moonwort, see Honesty				
Morning Glory			affection	G, K

FLOWER	OTHER COMMON NAME	BOTANICAL NAME	SENTIMENT	SOURCE
Morning Glory	Blue Convolvulus Minor	*Ipomoea nil* (Da)	repose	Da, G, K
Morus, see Mulberry Tree				
Moschatel, see Musk Plant				
Moss	Mossy Saxifrage		affection	G, K
Moss		*Sycopodium* (Ha)	ennui	G, Ha, K, N
Moss	Mossy Saxifrage	*Muscus* (M),	maternal love	A, Du, E, G, Ho, K,
		Sycopodium (E, P)		L, Le, M,N, O, P, .. T
Moss Rose, see Rose				
Moss Rosebud, see Rosebud				
Moss, English		*Sedum acre* (Da)	fortitude	Da
Moss, Ice/Iceland		*Cetraria islandica* (Wa)	health	G, Ho, L, O, Wa
Moss, Tall, see Lichen				
Mossy Saxifrage, see Moss				
Motherwort			concealed love, secret love	G, Ho, K, N, O, Wa..
Mountain Ash			prudence	G, Ho, K, L, N, O
Mountain Ash	Rowan Tree	*Pyrus aucuparia* (Wa)	talisman	Wa
Mountain Ash			with me you are safe	K
Mountain Laurel, see Laurel				
Mountain Mint, see Monarda				
Mountain Pink, see Pink				
Mourning Bride			I have lost all	G, K, N
Mourning Bride, see Scabious				
Mourning Geranium, see Geranium				
Mouse-eared Chickweed, see Chickweed				
Mouse-eared Forget Me not, see Forget Me Not				
Moving Plant	Quaking Grass		agitation	G, Ho, K, N, O
Mudwort			tranquility	G, K
Mudwort, Mugwort		*Artemisia vulgaris* (T)	happiness	K, N, T
Mulberry Tree, Black		*Morus nigra* (T)	I shall not survive you	Du, G, K, L, Le, O, T
Mulberry Tree, White		*Morus alba* (T)	wisdom	Du, G, Ho, K, L, Le, N, O, T
Mulberry, Red		*Morus rubra* (Wa)	wisdom	O, Wa
Mullein		*Verbascum thapsus* (Da)	good nature	Da, G, Ho, K, N, O
Multiflora Rose, see Rose				
Mushroom	Champignon	*Agaricus campestris* (T)	suspicion	G, Ho, K, L, N, O, T
Mushroom			I can't entirely trust you	G, K
Musk Plant		*Mimulus moschatus* (Da)	meeting, a meeting	Da
Musk Plant	Adoxa, Moschatel, Musk-Crowfoot	*Adoxa moschatellina* (T)	weakness, weak but winning	Du, G, Ho, K, L, Le, N, O, T
Musk Rose, see Rose				
Mustard, Mustard Seed		*Sinapis alba* (Da)	indifference	Da, G, K, N
Myosotis, see Forget Me Not				
Myrica, see Bayberry				
Myrobalan		*Prunus cerasifera* (T)	bereavement	T
Myrobalan	Indian Plum		privation	Du, G, K, L, Le, N, O
Myrrh			gladness	G, K, N
Myrtle		*Myrtus* (P), *Myrtus communis* (Da, T)	love	Da, Du, G, Ho, K, L, Le, N, O, P, T
Myrtle		*Myrtus* (E, Ha, P), *M. communis* (M)	love in absence	E, Ha, M, P

183

FLOWER	OTHER COMMON NAME	BOTANICAL NAME	SENTIMENT	SOURCE
Narcissus	Poet's Narcissus	*Narcissus poeticus*	egotism	G, Ha, Ho, K, L, M,
Narcissus		(Ha, M, P, T)		O, P, T
Narcissus, see also Daffodil, Jonquil	Poet's Narcissus	*Narcissus poeticus* (Ha, M)	self-love, self-esteem	Du, Ha, Le, M, N, P
Narcissus, False		*Narcissus pseudo-narcissus*	delusive hope	M, P.
		(M, P.)		
Narcissus, Yellow			disdain	T
Nardosmia, see Coltsfoot				
Nasturtium		*Tropeolum majus*	heroism	Da
Nasturtium		*Tropeolum* (E, P),	patriotism	A, E, G, Ha, K, N, P, O
		T. majus (Ha)		
Nasturtium	Scarlet Nasturtium		splendor	G, Ho, L, N
Nemophila			war-like trophy	N.
Nemophila		*Nemophila insignis* (Da)	prosperity	Da
Nepeta, see Ground Ivy			success everywhere	G, K.
Nerium, see Oleander				
Nettle	Stinging Nettle	*Urtica urens* (T)	cruelty	Du, Ho, L, Le, N, O, T
Nettle	Burning Nettle,	*Urtica* (Ha), *U. dioica* (Da)	slander	A, Da, G, Ha, Ho, K,
	Stinging Nettle			N
Nettle	Common Stinging Nettle		you are spiteful	K.
Nettle Tree			plan	N.
Nettle, Nettle Tree	Nettle Tree		conceit	G, K, N.
Nigella, see Love-in-a-Mist				
Night Convolvulus, see Convolvulus				
Night-blooming Cereus, see Cereus				
Night-smelling Geranium, see Geranium				
Nightshade				
Nightshade		*Solanum* (E), *S. nigrum* (Ha, P)	dark thoughts	A, E, Ha, P.
Nightshade	Deadly Nightshade	*Atropa belladonna* (Da)	death	Da
Nightshade	Deadly Nightshade		falsehood	K.
Nightshade		*Solanum nigrum* (P)	skepticism	N, P
Nightshade			sorcery, witchcraft	N.
Nightshade, see also Enchanter's Nightshade	Bittersweet Nightshade	*Solanum dulcamara* (T)	truth	Du, G, K, L, Le, N, O, T.
Norway Fir, see Pine				
Nosegay			gallantry	Du, L, Le, N, O
Nutmeg Geranium, see Geranium				
Nymphea, see Water Lily				
Oak		*Quercus alba* (Da)	honor	A.
Oak Leaf		*Quercus* (Ha, P)	bravery	G, Ha, K, P.
Oak Leaf		*Quercus* (Ha, P)	humanity	Ha, P.
Oak, Live		*Quercus virens* (Wa)	liberty	A, G, Ho, K, O, Wa.
Oak, Oak Tree		*Quercus* (E, P, Wa),	hospitality	Du, E, G, Ho, K, L,
		Q. pedunculata (T)		Le, P, O, T, Wa
Oak, White		*Quercus alba* (Wa)	independence	G, Ho, K, O, Wa
Oak-leaved Geranium, see Geranium				
Oats		*Avena sativa* (Da)	country life	A.
Oats		*Avena* (Ha), *A. sativa* (M)	music, the witching soul	G, Ha, Ho, K, M, O
			of music	
Ocimum, see Basil				
Oenothera, see Evening Primrose				
Olea, see Olive				
Oleander		*Nerium* (E), *N. oleander*	beware	A, E, G, Ho, K, M,
		(Da, M)		O, P

185

FLOWER	OTHER COMMON NAME	BOTANICAL NAME	SENTIMENT	SOURCE
Pea	Everlasting Pea		appointed meeting	A, G, Ho, K, N, O
Pea	Everlasting Pea		lasting pleasure	A, G, Ho, K, N, O
Pea, Everlasting		*Lathyrus latifolius* (E, Ha, M, P)	wilt thou go? wilt thou go away? wilt thou go with me?	E, Ha, M, P
Pea, Sweet			delicate pleasure	G, Ho, K, O
Pea, Sweet		*Lathyrus odoratus* (Da, E, Ha, M, P, Wa)	departure	Da, E, G, Ha, K, M, N, P, Wa
Peach			your qualities, like your charms, are unequalled	G, K
Peach Blossom		*Amygdalus* (E), *A. persica* (Ha, P), *Persica vulgaris* (Da)	I am your captive	Da, E, G, Ha, Ho, K, N, O, P
Peach Blossom			this heart is thine	A
Pear			affection	G, K
Pear Tree			comfort	G, K
Pelagorium, see Geranium				
Pennyroyal			flee away	G, Ho, K, N,
Penstemon		*Penstemon azureus* (K), *P. campanulatus* (Da)	high-bred	Da, K
Peony		*Peonia* (Ha)	anger	Ha
Peony		*Peonia officinalis* (Da, T)	bashful shame, shame	A, G, Ho, K, L, N, O, T
Peony			bashfulness	G, K, N
Peony		*Peonia* (E)	ostentation	E
Pepper Plant			satire	Ho, O
Peppermint		*Mentha piperita* (T)	cordiality, warmth of feeling or sentiment, warmth	Du, G, K, L, Le, N, T
Periwinkle	Blue Periwinkle, Red Periwinkle	*Vinca major* (Da), *V. minor* (Ha, P)	early friendship, early and sincere friendship	Da, G, Ha, K, N, P
Periwinkle	Blue Periwinkle, Red Periwinkle, White Periwinkle	*Vinca minor* (P, M, Wa), *V. rosea* (Ha)	pleasant/tender recollections, pleasures of memory, pleasing/sweet remembrance	A, Du, Ha, G, Ho, K, L, Le, M, N, O, P, T, Wa
Persian Lilac, see Lilac				
Persicaria		*Polygonum oriental* (Wa)	restoration	G, Ho, K, N, O, Wa
Persimmon		*Diospyros virginiana* (Da, Wa)	amid nature's beauties	Da, Wa
Persimmon			bury me amid nature's beauties	A, G, Ho, K, N, O
Peruvian Heliotrope, see Heliotrope				
Petunia		*Petunia argentea* (Da)	keep your promises	Da
Petunia		*Petunia* (E)	thou art less proud than they deem thee	A, E
Phalaris, see Grass				
Phaseolus	Scarlet Runner Bean	*Phaseolus multiflorus* (Da)	opportunity	Da
Pheasant's Eye, see Adonis				
Philadelphus, see Syringa				
Phlox		*Phlox* (E), *P. maculata* (A, M)	our souls are united	A, E
Phlox	Wild Sweet William	*Phlox subulata* (Da), *P. maculata* (Ha, P)	unanimity	Da, Ha, Ho, N, O, P
Phoradendron, see Mistletoe				
Physalis, see Winter Cherry				
Physostegia, see False Dragon Head				
Pigeon Berry			indifference	G, K
Pimpernel			change	G, K, LP
Pimpernel		*Anagallis arvensis* (Da)	mirth	Da
Pimpernel		*Anagallis arvensis* (T, Wa)	rendezvous, assignation	Ho, O, P, T, Wa

FLOWER	OTHER COMMON NAME	BOTANICAL NAME	SENTIMENT	SOURCE
Pine	Fir, Scotch Fir, Silver Fir	*Pinus sylvestris* (Wa)	elevation	Du, G, Ho, K, L, Le,. N, O, T, Wa
Pine	Pitch Pine	*Pinus* (E), *P. rigida* (P)	faith	E, P
Pine			heartiness	L
Pine	Pitch Pine	*Pinus rigida* Ha)	philosophy	Da, G, Ha, K, N
Pine	Black Spruce	*Pinus nigra* (Ha)	pity	A, G, Ha, Ho, K, N,. O
Pine	Fir, Pitch Pine	*Pinus* (E), *P. balsamea* (Ha), *P. rigida* (Ha, P)	time	E, G, Ha, Ho, K, N, . O, P
Pine Tree			daring	T
Pine, Spruce		*Abies nigra* (Da)	farewell	Da, N
Pine, Spruce	Spruce Pine, Norway Fir	*Pinus abies* (Ha, P)	hope in adversity	A, G, Ha, K, N, P
Pineapple		*Bromelia ananas* (T, Wa)	perfection, you are perfect	A, Du, G, Ho, K, L,. Le, N, O, T, Wa
Pinelia Cattleya, see Cattleya				
Pink			boldness	G, K, N
Pink	Yellow Carnation/Pink	*Dianthus* (P, Wa), *D. caryophyllus* (Da)	contempt, disdain	A, Da, Du, G, Ho, K, L, Le, N, O, P, Wa
Pink	Carnation		fascination	N
Pink	Dianthus		make haste	K
Pink	Double Red Carnation, Red Carnation	*Dianthus* (Wa), *D. prolifer* (T), *D. rubeus* (P)	lively and pure love/affection, pure and ardent love	G, Ho, K, L, N, O, P, T, Wa
Pink	Carnation	*Dianthus* (E)	pride	E
Pink	Carnation	*Dianthus* (Ha), *D. caryophyllus* (M)	pride and beauty	Ha, M
Pink	Single Carnation, Single Pink		pure love	Du, G, K, Le
Pink	Carnation		woman's love	N
Pink, China or Indian Pink	Single China Pink, Single Indian Pink	*Dianthus* (Wa)	aversion	G, Ho, K, N, O, Wa..
Pink, Deep Red	Deep Red Carnation		alas! for my poor heart	G, K
Pink, Double Indian	China Pink, Indian Pink	*Dianthus chinensis* (Ha)	always lovely, you will always be lovely	G, Ha, K, N
Pink, Double Red or Red Pink	Double Red Carnation, Red Carnation	*Dianthus rubeus* (E, Ha, M, P)	woman's love	A, E, G, Ha, K, M,. N, P
Pink, Garden			childishness	L
Pink, Indian				
Pink, Mountain		*Dianthus cesius* (Ha)	aspiring, you are aspiring	A, Ha, K, N
Pink, Striped	Variegated Pink		refusal	G, Ho, K, N, O
Pink, White			ingeniousness	G, K, N
Pink, White	White Carnation	*Dianthus albus* (E, M)	lovely and pure affection	E, M
Pink, White			talent	G, Ho, K, N, O
Pink, White or Variegated		*Dianthus albus* (Ha), *D. varietagus* (Ha)	you are fair and fascinating	Ha
Pink Bindweed, see Convolvulus				
Pink Larkspur, see Larkspur				
Pink Verbena, see Verbena				
Pitch Pine, see Pine				
Pitcher Plant		*Sarracenia psittacina* (Da)	instinct	Da
Plane Tree		*Platanus* (Wa), *P. orientalis* (T)	genius	Du, G, Ho, K, L, Le,. N, O, T, Wa
Plantain			white man's footsteps	K
Platanus, see Plane Tree				
Plum Tree		*Prunus domestica* (T)	fidelity	G, K, T
Plum Tree		*Prunus domestica* (Wa)	keep/perform your promises	Du, L, Le, N, O, Wa.

FLOWER	OTHER COMMON NAME	BOTANICAL NAME	SENTIMENT	SOURCE
Red Primrose, Rose-colored Primrose, see Primrose				
Red Rose, see Rose				
Red Rosebud, see Rosebud				
Red Salvia, see Salvia				
Red Tulip, see Tulip				
Red Valerian, see Valerian				
Red-leaved Rose, see Rose				
Reed	Common Reed		complaisance	G, Ho, K, N, O
Reed	Bundles of Reeds		music	A, Du, G, Ho, K, L, Le, N, O, T
Reed	Feathery Reed, Split Reed		indiscretion	G, K, L, N, T
Reed, Flowering	Flowering Reed, Flowering Rush	*Canna augustifolia* (E, Ha, M, P)	confidence in heaven	A, E, G, Ha, Ho, K, M, N, O, P
Reed, see Bulrush				
Reseda, see Dyer's Weed, Mignonette				
Rest Harrow		*Ononis spinosa* (T)	obstacle	L, N, T
Rest Harrow			patience	O
Rhododendron	Rosebay		beware	G, K, N
Rhododendron	Rosebay		danger	G, Ho, K, N, O
Rhododendron	Rosebay		dignity in misfortune	O
Rhododendron	Rosebay	*Rhododendron maximum* (Da)	talking	Da
Rhododendron, see Laurel				
Rhodora		*Rhodora canadensis* (Da)	beauty in retirement	Da
Rhubarb			advice	G, K, N
Rhus, see Sumac				
Richardia, see Calla Lily				
Robinia, see Acacia, Locust				
Rock Alyssum, see Alyssum				
Rock Madwort, see Madwort				
Rock Maple, see Maple				
Rock Rose, see Cistus				
Rocket	Dame's Violet, Queen's Rocket	*Hesperis matronalis* (Ha)	fashion, fashionable, she will be fashionable	G, Ha, K, N
Rocket			I burn	L
Rocket		*Hesperis matronalis* (Da)	rivalry	Da, G, Ho, K, N, O
Rocket	Queen's Rocket		you are the queen of coquettes	G, Ho, K, N, O
Rosa, see Rose				
Rose	Full-blown Rose, Full Red Rose	*Rosa* (Wa), *R. rubifolia* (P)	beauty	A, Ho L, N, O, P, T, Wa
Rose	Eglantine, Sweetbrier	*Rosa rubiginosa* (Da)	home	Da
Rose	Eglantine, Sweetbriar	*Rosa rubignosa* (Ha, M, P)	I wound to heal	G, Ha, K, M, N, P
Rose	Red Rose		love	Du, G, K, Le, N
Rose Acacia, see Acacia				
Rose, Austrian		*Rosa bicolor* (Ha, M, P), *R. eglanteria* (Da)	loveliness, thou art all that is lovely, thou art very lovely	Da, G, K, Ha, M, N, P
Rose Balm, see Balm				
Rose, Bridal		*Rubus rosafolius* (E, Ha, M, P)	happy love	E, G, K, Ha, M, N, P
Rose Bush in the Middle of a Mound			good company	L
Rose, Burgundy		*Rosa parvifolia* (E, Ha)	simplicity and beauty	E, Ha
Rose, Burgundy			unconscious beauty	G, K, N
Rose, Cabbage			ambassador of love	G, K, N
Rose Campion, see Campion, Corn Cockle				
Rose, Carolina		*Rosa carolina* (Ha)	love is dangerous	G, Ha, K, N

FLOWER	OTHER COMMON NAME	BOTANICAL NAME	SENTIMENT	SOURCE
Rose, China	Monthly Rose		beauty always/ever new	Du, G, L, Le, Ho, K, N, O, Wa
Rose, China/Multiflora	Multiflora Rose	*Rosa multiflora* (Wa)	charms, many charms	Wa
Rose, China or Multiflora	Multiflora Rose	*Rosa multiflora* (E, Ha, M)	grace	E, G, Ha, K, M
Rose, China, Dark		*Rosa semperflorens* (Ha)	forsaken	Ha
Rose, Christmas			tranquilize my anxiety	G, K, N
Rose, Christmas, see Christmas Rose				
Rose, Daily		*Rosa quotidiana* (Ha)	lightness	Ha
Rose, Daily			thy smile I aspire to	G, K, N
Rose, Damask		*Rosa damascena* (E, Ha, M)	bashful love	E, Ha, M
Rose, Damask		*Rosa damascena* (T)	beauty ever new	T
Rose, Damask		*Rosa damascena* (Da)	blushing beauty	Da
Rose, Damask			brilliant complexion, freshness of complexion	G, Ho, K, N, O
Rose, Damask		*Rosa damascena* (Ha)	youth	Ha
Rose, Damask				
Rose, Deep Red		*Rosa rubra* (Ha, P)	bashful shame, sensitive modesty	G, Ha, K, N, P
Rose, Dog			passionate, platonic, or pure love	Du, E, G, Ho, K, L, Le, N, P, T, Wa
Rose, Dog			pleasure and pain	G
Rose, Dog			love, pleasure and pain	N
Rose, Dog		*Rosa canina* (T)	simplicity	O, T
Rose, Dried White			death preferable to loss of innocence	G, Ho, K, O
Rose, Eglantine/Sweetbriar, see Eglantine				
Rose, Full-blown	Full-blown Rose, Placed Over Two Buds		secrecy	G, K, N
Rose, Hundred-leaved		*Rosa centifolia* (Ha)	dignity of mind	Ha, G, K
Rose, Hundred-leaved		*Rosa centifolia* (Wa)	grace, the graces	Du, Ho, L, Le, O, T, Wa
Rose, Hundred-leaved			pride	G, K, N
Rose, Japan			beauty is your only attraction	G, Ho, K, N, O
Rose, Lancaster			union	N
Rose Leaf			I am never importunate	T
Rose Leaf			I will not trouble you	O
Rose Leaf			you may hope	K
Rose, Maiden-blush			if you love me, you will find it out	G, K, N
Rose, May			precocity	Ho, N, O
Rose, Monthly, see Rose, China				
Rose, Moss		*Rosa muscosa* (T)	love	L, T
Rose, Moss			pleasure without alloy	O, Wa
Rose, Moss	Full Moss Rose	*Rosa muscosa* (E, Ha, M, P)	superior merit	E, Ha, M, N, P
Rose, Moss			voluptuous love	Ho
Rose, Moss		*Rosa muscosa* (T)	voluptuousness	L, T
Rose Mundi			variety	G, K, N
Rose Mundi		*Rosa versicolor* (Ha)	you are merry	Ha, N
Rose, Musk		*Rosa moschata* (T)	capricious beauty	Du, G, Ho, K, L, Le, N, T, Wa
Rose, Musk	Musk Rose Cluster	*Rosa moschata* (Ha)	charming	G, Ha, K, N
Rose, Musk		*Rosa moschata* (Da)	charms of home	Da
Rose of Japan, see Camellia Japonica				
Rose, Pompon			genteel, gentility	Ho, L, N
Rose, Pompon			kindness	Ho, L, N

FLOWER	OTHER COMMON NAME	BOTANICAL NAME	SENTIMENT	SOURCE
Rose, Pompon		*Rosa moschata pomponia* (T)	loveliness, pretty, prettiness	Ho, L, N, T
Rose, Red-leaved		*Rosa rubrifolia* (Ha)	beauty and prosperity	Ha, N
Rose, Red-leaved		*Rosa rubrifolia* (E)	diffidence	E
Rose, Single			simplicity	Du, G, K, L, Le
Rose, Thornless			early attachment	G, K, N
Rose, Thornless		*Rosa inermis* (Ha)	ingratitude	Ha
Rose, Unique			call me not beautiful	G, K, N
Rose, White	Full White Rose		I am worthy of you	G, K, N
Rose, White		*Rosa alba* (Ha, M)	sadness	Ha, M
Rose, White		*Rosa alba* (Da)	secrecy	Da
Rose, White			silence	Du, L, Le, O, T, Wa
Rose, White		*Rosa alba* (E)	too young to love	E
Rose, White and Red			unity	G, K, N
Rose, White and Red				
Rose, White with Red			fire or warmth of the heart	L, T
Rose, Wild			simplicity	O, Wa
Rose, Withered			fleeting beauty	Du, Le
Rose, Withered White		*Rosa alba* (Ha)	I am in despair	Ha
Rose, Withered White			transient impressions	G, K, N
Rose, Yellow		*Rosa lutea* (M, Wa)	infidelity, unfaithfulness	Du, Ho, L, Le, M, O, T, Wa
Rose, Yellow			jealousy	G, K, N
Rose, Yellow		*Rosa lutea* (Ha)	let us forget	Ha
Rose, Yellow	Yellow Sweetbriar		decrease of love	G, K, N
Rose, York and Lancaster		*Rosa versicola* (Ha)	war	G, Ha, K, N
Rosebay, see Rhododendron				
Rosebud	Moss Rosebud	*Rosa* (E), *R. moscosa* (Ha, P)	confession, confession of love	E, G, Ha, K, N, P
Rosebud	Red Rosebud		young girl, you are young and beautiful	Du, L, Le, N, T, Wa
Rosebud			youthful charms	O
Rosebud, Red		*Rosa rubrifolia* (Ha)	pure and lovely, may you ever be pure and lovely	G, Ha, K
Rosebud, White			girlhood	G, K
Rosebud, White			heart unacquainted with/ ignorant of love, the heart that knows not love	Du, G, Ho, K, L, Le, N, O, Wa
Rosebud, White		*Rosa alba* (Ha)	too young to love	Ha
Rose-leaved Rubus, see Rubus				
Roses, Crown/Garland/Wreath of			reward of merit/virtue	G, Ho, K, L, N, O, T
Rose-scented Geranium, see Geranium				
Rosemary			fidelity	Ho
Rosemary		*Rosmarinus officinalis* (Da, Ha, M)	remembrance	A, Da, G, Ha, K, M, N, P
Rosemary		*Rosmarinus* (Wa), *R. officinalis* (T)	your presence revives me	Du, L, Le, N, O,T, Wa
Rowan Tree, see Mountain Ash				
Royal Fern, see Fern				
Rubia, see Madder				
Rubus, see Bramble, Rose				
Rubus, Rose-leaved		*Rubus rosefolius* (Da)	threats	Da
Rudbeckia		*Rudbeckia laciniata* (Da)	justice	Da, G, Ho, K, N, O
Rue		*Ruta graveolens* (Ha)	disdain	G, Ha, K, N
Rue		*Ruta graveolens* (Wa)	grace	Ho, O, Wa
Rue		*Ruta graveolens* (Wa)	purification	Ho, O, Wa
Rue		*Ruta graveolens* (Da)	repentance	Da

FLOWER	OTHER COMMON NAME	BOTANICAL NAME	SENTIMENT	SOURCE
Rue, Wild			manners, morals	Du, L, Le, T
Rumex, see Dock				
Rush, Flowering, see Reed				
Rush, see Bulrush				
Ruta, see Rue				
Rye Grass			changeable disposition	G, K
Sabatia, see Star Flower				
Saffron		*Carthamus tinctorius* (Ha)	marriage	Ha, N
Saffron Flower			do not abuse	Ho, L, N
Saffron Flower			excess is dangerous,	A, Du, G, K, Le, N, .
			beware of excess	O
Saffron, see also Crocus				
Sage		*Salvia* (E),	domestic virtue	Da, E, G, Ha, K, M,.
		S. officinalis (Da, Ha, M)		N
Sage	Garden Sage	*Salvia officinalis* (T)	esteem	Du, G, Ho, K, L, Le,.
				N, O, T
Sagebrush			good luck, happiness	L
Sainfoin	Shaking Sainfoil	*Hedysarum gyrans* (T)	agitation	Du, G, K, L, Le, O, T
Saint John's Wort		*Hypericum* (Ha, M, P)	animosity	G, Ha, K, M, P
Saint John's Wort		*Hypericum* (P)	superstition	Du, G, K, Le, N, P
Saint John's Wort			superstitious sanctity	Ho, O
Saint John's Wort			you are a prophet	N
Salix, see Osier, Willow				
Salvia	Scarlet Sage, Red Salvia	*Salvia splendens* (Da)	energy	Da, K
Salvia, Blue			wisdom	K
Salvia, see also Sage				
Sambucus, see Elder				
Saponaria, see Bouncing Bess				
Sarsaparilla		*Smilax sarsaparilla* (Da)	experience	Da
Sardonia, Sardony			irony	Du, G, L, Le, N, O,.
Sarracenia, see Pitcher Plant				
Sassafras		*Sassafras officinale* (Da)	favor	Da
Satin Flower			sincerity	N
Satin Flower, see Honesty				
Satureia, see Summer Savory				
Saxifraga, Silene, see London Pride				
Scabious	Mourning Bride,	*Scabiosa atropurpurea*	unfortunate attachment	Da, G,Ha, Ho, K, N, .
	Sweet Scabious	(Da, Ha, P)		O, P
Scabious, Sweet			widowhood	G, K, N, P
Scarlet Auricula, see Auricula				
Scarlet Fuchsia, see Fuchsia				
Scarlet Geranium, see Geranium				
Scarlet Ipomoea, see Ipomoea				
Scarlet Lily, see Lily				
Scarlet Lychnis, see Lychnis				
Scarlet Nasturtium, see Nasturtium				
Scarlet Sage or Red Salvia, see Salvia				
Scarlet Verbena, see Verbena				
Scarlet or Wild Poppy, see Poppy				
Schinus			religious enthusiasm	G, K
Scilla, see Hyacinth				
Scorpion Grass, see Forget Me Not				
Scotch Fir, see Pine				
Scotch Thistle, see Thistle				

193

FLOWER	OTHER COMMON NAME	BOTANICAL NAME	SENTIMENT	SOURCE
Scratch Weed, see Bed Straw				
Scirpus, see Bulrush				
Sea Bindweed, see Convolvulus				
Sea Lavender			dauntlessness	N
Sea Thrift, see Statice				
Sedum, see Moss, Stonecrop				
Sempervivum, see Houseleek				
Sensitive Plant		*Mimosa pudica* (Da), *M. sensitiva* (T)	bashful modesty, bashfulness, modesty, timidity	Da, Ho, L, O, T
Sensitive Plant			chastity	Du, Le
Sensitive Plant			delicate feelings	K
Sensitive Plant, see also Mimosa				
Senvy			indifference	G, K, N
Serpentine Cactus, see Cactus				
Service Tree		*Pyrus domestica* (T)	prudence	N, O, T
Service Tree			accord, harmony	L
Shaking Sainfoil, see Sainfoin				
Shamrock, see Clover				
Shell Flower, see Balm				
Shepherd's Purse			I offer you my all	K
Siberian Crab Tree Blossom, see Crab Tree Blossom				
Sidesaddle Flower			will you pledge me?	O
Silene, see Catchfly				
Silver Fir, see Pine				
Silver-leaved Geranium, see Geranium				
Simlax, see Jacob's Ladder				
Sinapis, see Mustard, Mustard Seed				
Single Carnation/Pink, see Pink				
Single China Aster, see Aster				
Single China/Indian Pink, see Pink				
Single Rose, see Rose				
Single-Flowered Larkspur, see Larkspur				
Small Bindweed, see Convolvulus				
Small Cape Marigold, see Marigold				
Small White Violet, see Violet				
Smilax, see Sarsaparilla				
Snake Cactus, see Cactus				
Snake's Lounge			slander	N
Snakesfoot			horror	G, K, L, N
Snapdragon			no	K
Snapdragon		*Antirrhinum majus* (Da, T)	presumption	Da, Du, G, Ho, K, L, Le, N, T
Snapdragon		*Anthirrinum* (E)	you are dazzling, but dangerous	A, E, O
Snowball	Guelder Rose, Viburnum		age	G, Ho, K, O, N
Snowball	Guelder Rose, Viburnum		bound	G, K, N
Snowball	Guelder Rose, Snowball Tree	*Viburnum opulus* (T)	good news	T
Snowball	Guelder Rose	*Viburnum* (E), *V. opulus* (Ha), *V. roseum* (Da)	thoughts of heaven	A, Da, E, Ha, Ho, O
Snowball	Guelder Rose, Viburnum		winter	A, G, Ho, K, O
Snowball	Guelder Rose, Viburnum		winter of age	N
Snowdrop		*Galanthus* (Wa)	consolation	Da, Ho, L, M, N, O, T, Wa

FLOWER	OTHER COMMON NAME	BOTANICAL NAME	SENTIMENT	SOURCE
Snowdrop		*Galanthus nivalis* (Ha, P)	friend in need, friendship in adversity	Ha, P
Snowdrop		*Galanthus nivalis* (P)	hope	Du, G, K, L, N, P
Snowdrop		*Galanthus* (E)	I am not a summer friend	E
Snowdrop Tree		*Halesia diptera* (Da)	exhilaration	Da
Solanum, see Nightshade, Potato				
Solidago, see Golden Rod				
Sorghum	Broom Corn	*Sorghum vulgare* (Da)	labor	Da
Sorrel			affection	G, K
Sorrel			wit	A
Sorrel	Wild Sorrel		wit ill-timed	G, Ho, K, N, O
Sorrel, Wild		*Oxalis* (Ha), *O. floribunda* (Da)	parental affection	A, Da, Ha, N
Sorrel, Wood		*Oxalis* (Wa), *O. acetosella* (T)	joy	A, Du, G, K, L, Le, N, O, T, Wa
Sorrel, Wood		*Oxalis* (Ha)	maternal tenderness	G, Ha, Ho, K, N
Southernwood		*Artemisia abrotanum* (Da)	bantering, jest, jesting	Da, G, K, N, O
Sowbread			diffidence	N
Spanish Jasmine, see Jasmine				
Spearmint			warmth of sentiment	G, K, N
Speedwell		*Veronica* (Ha), *V. arvensis* (Da, Wa)Wa	female fidelity	Da, G, Ha, K, L, N, P
Speedwell	Veronica, Wall Speedwell	*Veronica* (Ha, M), *V. arvensis* (Da, Wa)	fidelity	Du, Ho, L, Le, M, O, P, Wa
Speedwell, Germander			facility	G, K, N
Speedwell, Germander		*Veronica chamaedrys* (T)	faithfulness	T
Speedwell, Spiked			resemblance, semblance	G, Ho, K, O
Spider Ophrys, see Ophrys				
Spiderwort			esteem, not love	G, K, N
Spiderwort	Virginia Spiderwort	*Tradescantia virginica* (Da, T), *Anthericum* (Wa)	momentary/transient happiness	Da, G, Ho, O, T, Wa
Spiderwort			transient love	N, O
Spiked Speedwell, see Speedwell				
Spikenard		*Aralia racemosa* (Da)	benefits	Da
Spindle Tree		*Euonymus europea* (T)	your image is engraven on my heart, your charms are engraven/traced on my heart	A, Du, G, K, L, Le, N, O, T
Spiraea, see Meadowsweet				
Split Reed, see Reed				
Spotted Arum, see Arum				
Sprig of Ivy with Tendrils, see Ivy				
Spring Crocus, see Crocus				
Spruce Pine, see Pine				
Spurge Laurel, see Daphne				
Squirting Cucumber, see Cucumber				
Standing Cypress, see Ipomopsis				
Stapelia	Carion Flower	*Stapelia bufonia* (Da)	offense	Da
Staphylea, see Bladdernut				
Star Flower		*Sabatia brachiata* (Da)	reciprocity	Da
Star of Bethlehem			follow me	O
Star of Bethlehem		*Ornithogalum* (P)	guidance	N, P
Star of Bethlehem		*Ornithogalum* (E)	let us follow Jesus	E
Star of Bethlehem		*Ornithogalum umbellatum* (M)	the light of our path	Ho, M, O
Star of Bethlehem		*Ornithogalum umbellatum* (T)	purity	Du, G, K, L, Le, T
Star of Bethlehem		*Ornithogalum* (Ha, P), *O. umbellatum* (Da)	reconciliation	Da, Ha, P

FLOWER	OTHER COMMON NAME	BOTANICAL NAME	SENTIMENT	SOURCE
Starwort, see Aster				
Statice	Sea Thrift, Statice Maritime	*Statice maritima* (T)	sympathy	L, T
Stellaria, see Chickweed				
Stephanotis			will you accompany me to the East?	K
Stinging Nettle, see Nettle				
Stock, see Wallflower				
Stock, Ten-week	Mahon's Stock	*Matthiola annua* (Da, T)	promptness, promptitude	Da, Du, G, Ho, K, L, Le, N, O, T
Stonecrop	Sedum		tranquility	Du, G, K, Le, N
Stramonium, see Datura				
Straw, Broken			dissension	O, T
Straw, Broken			rupture, rupture of a contract	Du, G, K, L, Le, N, O, T
Straw, Whole			union	Du, G, K, L, Le
Strawberry		*Fragaria* (E), *F. vesca* (Da, T)	perfect excellence/goodness, perfection	Da, Du, E, Ho, L, Le, N, O, P, T
Strawberry Blossom			foresight	K
Strawberry Tomato, see Winter Cherry				
Strawberry Tree			esteem and love	N
Strawberry Tree			esteem, not love	G, K
Strawberry Tree		*Arbutus unedo* (Wa)	perseverance	Wa
Strawberry-tree, see Arbutus				
Striped Carnation, see Pink				
Succory, see Chicory				
Sultan, Lilac			I forgive you	K
Sultan, White			sweetness	K
Sultan, Yellow			contempt	K
Sumac		*Rhus* (E)	splendid misery	E
Sumac	Venice Sumac	*Rhus aromatica* (Da)	splendor	Da, G, Ho, K, O
Sumac, Venice		*Rhus cotinus* (Ha)	intellectual excellence	G, Ha, K
Summer Cypress, see Belvedere				
Summer Savory		*Satureia hortensis* (Da)	success	Da
Sunflower	Dwarf Sunflower	*Helianthus indicus* (P)	false riches	Le, P
Sunflower	Tall Sunflower		false riches	Du, Ho, K, L, T
Sunflower	Tall Sunflower	*Helianthus annus* (Da, Ha, Wa)	lofty thoughts, lofty and pure thoughts	Da, Ha, Wa
Sunflower		*Helianthus* (E)	smile on me still	E, O
Sunflower			you are my divinity	L
Sunflower, Dwarf		*Helianthus indicus* (Ha, M, P)	adoration, your devout adorer	G, Ha, K, M, N, P
Sunflower, Tall			haughtiness	G, K, N
Superb Lily, see Lily				
Swallowwort, see Butterfly Weed				
Swamp Magnolia, see Magnolia				
Sweet Alyssum, see Alyssum				
Sweet Balm, see Balm				
Sweet Basil, see Basil				
Sweet Bay, see Laurel				
Sweet Flag		*Acorus calamus* (Da, Wa)	fitness	Da, Ho, N, O, Wa
Sweet Marjoram, see Marjoram				
Sweet Pea, see Pea				
Sweet Potato		*Batatas edulis* (Da)	hidden qualities	Da
Sweet Scabious, see Scabious				
Sweet Sedge, see Indian Cress				
Sweet Sultan	Centaury		congratulations	N

FLOWER	OTHER COMMON NAME	BOTANICAL NAME	SENTIMENT	SOURCE
Sweet Sultan	Centaury	*Amerboa moschata* (Da), *Cen-taurea moschata* (T, Wa)	felicity, happiness	Da, Du, G, Ho, K, L, Le, N, O, T, W
Sweet Sultan Flower			widowhood	N
Sweet Violet, see Violet				
Sweet William		*Dianthus barbatus* (Wa)	childhood	Wa
Sweet William			craftiness	Ho, O
Sweet William			dexterity	K
Sweet William			finesse	Du, L, Le, N
Sweet William		*Dianthus barbatus* (E)	gallantry	E, G, K, N
Sweet William		*Dianthus barbatus* (Ha)	smile, a smile	Ha, N
Sweet William		*Dianthus barbatus* (Da)	stratagem	Da
Sweet-scented Clover, see Melilot				
Sweet-scented Coltsfoot, see Coltsfoot				
Sweetbriar, see Eglantine				
Sycamore			curiosity	Du, G, K, L, N
Sycamore		*Acer pseudoplatanus* (T)	reserve	T
Sycamore		*Acer pseudoplatanus* (Wa), *Platanus occidentalis* (Da)	woodland beauty	Da, Ho, O, Wa
Sycopodium, see Moss				
Syrian Mallow, see Mallow				
Syringa		Mock Orange	counterfeit	O
Syringa	Carolina Syringa, Mock Orange	*Philadelphus inodorus* (Ha)	disappointment	G, Ha, K, N
Syringa	Mock Orange	*Philadelphus coronarius* (T)	fraternal affection/love/ sympathy	Du, K, L, Le, T
Syringa	Carolina Syringa, Mock Orange	*Philadelphus* (Wa), *P. coron- arius* (Da), *P. inodorus* (E)	memory	A, Da, E, G, K, Ho, N, O, Wa
Syringa, see Lilac				
Tagetes, see Marigold				
Tall Moss, see Lichen				
Tall Sunflower, see Sunflower				
Tamarisk		*Tamarix* (Wa)	crime	G, Ho, K, N, O, Wa
Tamus, see Black Bryony				
Tanacetum, see Tansy				
Tansy		*Tanacetum* (Wa), *T. vulgare* (Da)	resistance	Da, Ho, O, Wa
Tansy, Wild			I declare war against you	Du, G, K, Le, N
Taraxacum, see Dandelion				
Tares, see Darnel				
Taxodium, see Cypress				
Taxus, see Yew				
Teasel	Fuller's Teasel	*Dipsacus* (Wa), *D. fullonum* (Da, T)	misanthropy	Da, G, Ho, K, L, Le, O, T, Wa
Teasel, Fuller's			austerity	Ho, O
Teasel, Fuller's			importunity	N
Tecoma, see Trumpet Flower				
Ten-week Stock, see Stock				
Tendrils of Climbing Plants			ties	Du, G, K, Le, N
Thistle		*Carduus* (Wa), *Cirsium arvense* (Da)	austerity	Da, G, K, L, N, O, Wa
Thistle			importunity	Ho, O
Thistle			independence	K
Thistle		*Carduus cimeolatus* (Ha2)	misanthropy	Du, G, Ha2, K
Thistle		*Carduus* (E)	never forget	E

197

FLOWER	OTHER COMMON NAME	BOTANICAL NAME	SENTIMENT	SOURCE
Thistle		*Carduus nutans* (T)	sternness	T
Thistle			surliness	Du, L
Thistle, Scotch			retaliation	G, K, N
Thistle Seed Head			depart	K
Thorn Apple, see Datura				
Thorn, Evergreen			solace in adversity	O
Thornless Rose, see Rose				
Thorn, Branch of			rigor	G, Ho, K, O
Thorn, Branch of			severity	G, Ho, K, N, O
Three-colored Indian Cress, see Indian Cress				
Thrift		*Armeria vulgaris* (Da)	sympathy	A, Da, Du, G, K, Le, N, O
Throatwort			neglected beauty	G, Ho, K, N, O
Thuja, see Arbor Vitae				
Thyme		*Thymus* (Wa), *Thymus serphyllum* (T)	activity	Du, G, Ho, K, L, Le, N, O, T, Wa
Thyme			courage	K
Thyme		*Thymus serpyllum* (Ha)	thriftiness	Ha
Tiger Flower		*Cigridia pavonia* (Da)	for once may pride befriend thee, pride befriend me	A, Da, G, Ho, K, N, O
Tilia, see Linden/Lime Tree				
Tofieldia, see Asphodel				
Toothwort		*Lathrea squamaria* (T)	concealment	T
Toothwort			secret love	N
Touch-me-not, see Balsam				
Tradescantia, see Spiderwort				
Trailing Arbutus	Arbutus, Mayflower	*Epigea repens* (Da)	simplicity	Da
Traveler's Joy, see Clematis				
Tree of Life			old age	G, Ho, K, O
Tree of Life, see Arbor Vitae				
Trefoil, see Clover				
Trembling Poplar, see Poplar				
Tremella	Trembling Grass, Tremella Nostoc		opposition, resistance	Du, G, K, L, Le, N, T
Tremella Nostoc			resolve the riddle	O
Trifolium, see Clover				
Trillium Pictum			modest beauty	G, K
Trillium Spinosum			be prudent	K
Triticum, see Wheat				
Tropeolum, see Indian Cress, Nasturtium				
Truffle			surprise	Du, G, K, L, Le, N, O
Trumpet Flower		*Tecoma radicans* (Da)	fame	Da, G, K
Trumpet Flower	Ash-leaved Trumpet Flower	*Bignonia radicans* (Wa)	separation	G, Ho, K, O, Wa
Trumpet Honeysuckle, see Honeysuckle				
Tuberose		*Polyanthus tuberosa* (Ha2, P)	sweet voice, a sweet voice	Ha2, P
Tuberose		*Polyanthus tuberosa* (Da, T, Wa)	voluptuousness	Da, L, T
Tuberose		*Polyanthus tuberosa* (P)	dangerous pleasures	Du, G, K, L, N, P, Wa
Tulip	Variegated Tulip	*Tulipa* (Ha, P)	beautiful eyes	E, G, Ha2, K, N, P
Tulip			charity	K

FLOWER	OTHER COMMON NAME	BOTANICAL NAME	SENTIMENT	SOURCE
Tulip	Red Tulip	*Tulipa* (P, Wa), *T. gesneriana*	declaration of love	A, Da, Du, G, Ha,
		(Da, Ha, M), *T. sylvestris* (T)		Ho, K,L, Le, M,
				N, O, P, T, Wa
Tulip	Tulip Tree	*Liriodendron tulipifera* (Ha)	fame	G, Ha, N
Tulip Tree		*Liriodendron tulipifera* (Wa)	rural happiness	A, Wa
Tulip, Yellow			hopeless love	G, K, N
Tumble Mustard			safety, security	L
Turnip			charity	G, Ho, N, O.
Tussilago, see Coltsfoot				
Ulmus, see Elm				
Unique Rose, see Rose				
Urtica, see Nettle				
Usrea, see Lichen				
Vaccinium, see Whortleberry				
Valerian	Red Valerian	*Valeriana montana* (T), *V.*	accommodating or obliging	Da, Du, G, Ho, K,
		rubra (Wa), *V. sylvatica* (Da)	disposition, readiness	Le, N, O, T
Valerian, Greek	Greek Valerian, Blue-	*Polemonium caeruleum* (T)	rupture	Du, G, Ho, K, L, Le,
	flowered Greek Valerian			
Valerian, Red	Red Valerian		facility	L
Variegated Carnation/Pink, see Pink				
Variegated Tulip, see Tulip				
Venetian Mallow, see Hibiscus				
Venice Sumac, see Sumac				
Venus's Car			fly with me	G, K, O
Venus's Flytrap	White Flytrap	*Dionea muscipula* (Da, Wa)	deceit	Da, G, Ho, K, Wa
Venus's Flytrap			have I caught you at last?	A, O
Venus's Looking Glass		*Campanula speculum* (T),	flattery	A, Da, Du, G, Ho, K,
		Specularia speculum (Da)		L, Le, N, O
Venus's Looking Glass				
Verbascum, see Mullein				
Verbena	Vervain	*Verbena* (E), *V. aubletia* (Da),	sensibility	Da, E, Ho, M, O
		V. fastata (M)		
Verbena	Vervain		sensitiveness	P
Verbena, Lemon	Aloysia	*Aloysia citriodora* (Da)	forgiveness	Da
Verbena, Pink			family union	K
Verbena, Scarlet			church unity, unite against evil	K
Verbena, White			pray for me	K
Verbena, see also Vervain				
Vernal Grass, see Grass				
Veronica Speciosa			keep this for my sake	K
Veronica, see Speedwell				
Vervain	Holly Herb	*Verbena officinalis* (T)	enchantment	Du, G, K, L, Le, N,
				O, T
Vervain		*Verbena* (Wa)	superstition	Ho, Wa
Vetch			shyness	N
Viburnum, see Laurestine, Snowball				
Vinca, see Periwinkle				
Vine		*Vitis vinifera* (T)	drunkenness, intoxication	Du, G, Ho, K, L, Le,
				N, O, T
Viola, see Pansy, Violet				
Violet	Blue Violet	*Viola* (E), *V. odorata* (Ha, P)	faith, faithfulness	E, G, Ha, K, N, P

FLOWER	OTHER COMMON NAME	BOTANICAL NAME	SENTIMENT	SOURCE
Violet	White or Sweet Violet	*Viola* (M, Wa), *V. blanda*	modesty	Da, Du, G, Ha, Ho,
		(Ha), *V. odorata* (Da, T)		K, L, Le, M, N, O,
				P, T, Wa
Violet, Blue			love	N
Violet, Dame			watchfulness	G, K
Violet, Purple			you occupy my thoughts	N
Violet, Small White			innocence and candor	Ho
Violet, White		*Viola lactea* (Wa)	candor	Du, L, Le, O, P, T, Wa
Violet, White			innocence	Du, Le, N, O, P
Violet, White			purity of sentiment	Ho
Violet, Yellow		*Viola nuttallii* (Ha)	rural happiness	G, Ha, K
Virgin's Bower, see Clematis				
Virginia Cactus, see Cactus				
Virginia Creeper			I cling to you both in sunshine and shade	K
Virginia Jasmine, see Jasmine				
Virginia Juniper, see Cedar				
Virginia Spiderwort, see Spiderwort				
Viscaria Oculata			will you dance with me?	K
Viscum, see Mistletoe				
Vitex, see Agnus Castus				
Vitis, see Grape, Vine				
Volkameria	Volkameria Japonica		may you be happy	A, G, Ho, K, O
Wake Robin, see Arum				
Walking Fern, see Fern				
Wall Speedwell, see Speedwell				
Wallflower	Gillyflower	*Cheiranthus incanus* (M)	bonds of affection	G, Ho, K, M, N
Wallflower	Gillyflower	*Cheiranthus* (E, Wa), *C. cheiri* (Da, Ha2, M, P), *C. fruticulosus* (T)	faithfulness/fidelity in adversity/misfortune	Da, Du, E, G, Ha2, Ho, K, L, Le, M, N, O, P, T, Wa
Wallflower	Garden Stock, Gillyflower, Stock	*Cheiranthus* (E), *C. cheiri* (T), *C. incanus* (P, Wa)	lasting beauty	Du, E, G, Ho, K, L, Le, N, O, P, T, Wa
Wallflower	Garden Stock, Gillyflower	*Cheiranthus incanus* (Ha)	she is fair	Ha, P
Wallflower				
Walnut	Black Walnut	*Juglans nigra* (Da, Wa)	intellect	Da, G, Ho, K, N, O, Wa
Walnut			stratagem	Du, G, K, Le, N
Walnut	White Walnut	*Juglans cinerea* (Da)	understanding	Da
Watcher by the Wayside			never despair	K
Water Lily	Lotus, White Water Lily	*Lotus* (P), *Nymphea* (E, M), *N. alba* (T, Wa), *N. odorata* (Da)	eloquence	Da, Du, E, G, K, L, Le, M, N, O, P, Wa
Water Lily	Lotus Flower	*Lotus* (Ha, P, Wa)	estranged love	G, Ha, K, N, P, Wa
Water Lily	White Water Lily	*Nymphea odorata* (Ha2), *N. alba* (Ha)	purity of heart	G, Ha2, K
Water Lily	Lotus		repose	K
Water Lily	Lotus Flower		silence	Ho, O
Water Lily Leaf	Lotus Leaf		recantation	G, K, N
Water Star			beauty combined with piety	O
Watermelon	Melon		bulkiness	G, Ho, K, O
Wax Myrtle, see Bayberry				
Wax Plant			susceptibility	G, Ho, K, O
Weeping Willow, see Willow				

FLOWER	OTHER COMMON NAME	BOTANICAL NAME	SENTIMENT	SOURCE
Wheat	Wheat Stalk	*Triticum* (Wa), *T. caninum* (Ha2), *T. vulgare* (Da)	prosperity, riches	Da, G, Ha2, Ho, K, L, N, O, T, Wa
Whin, see Broom				
White Acacia, see Acacia				
White Camellia, see Camellia				
White Carnation/Pink, see Pink				
White Catchfly, see Catchfly				
White Cherry Tree, see Cherry Tree				
White Chrysanthemum, see Chrysanthemum				
White Clover, see Clover				
White Daisy, see Daisy				
White Dittany of Crete, see Dittany of Crete				
White Heather, see Heather				
White Jasmine, see Jasmine				
White Julienne, see Julienne				
White Lilac, see Lilac				
White Lily, see Lily				
White Mulberry Tree, see Mulberry				
White Oak, see Oak				
White Periwinkle, see Periwinkle				
White Poplar, see Poplar				
White Poppy, see Poppy				
White Rose, see Rose				
White Rosebud, see Rosebud				
White Verbena, see Verbena				
White Violet, see Violet				
White Walnut, see Walnut				
White Water Lily, see Water Lily				
Whole Straw, see Straw				
Whortleberry	Bilberry	*Vaccinium myrtillus* (T, Wa)	treachery, treason	A, Du, G, K, L, Le, N, O, T, Wa
Wicker, see Osier				
Wild Balm, see Monarda				
Wild Daisy, see Daisy				
Wild Dogwood, see Dogwood				
Wild Geranium, see Geranium				
Wild Grape, see Grape				
Wild Honeysuckle, see Honeysuckle				
Wild Plum Tree, see Plum				
Wild Rose, see Rose				
Wild Rue, see Rue				
Wild Sorrel, see Sorrel				
Willow		*Salix* (E), *S.babylonica* (Wa)	forsaken	E, Ho, N, Wa
Willow	Weeping Willow, Willow of Babylon	*Salix babylonica* (Ha2, M)	forsaken lover	Ha2, M, O
Willow, Creeping			love forsaken	G, K
Willow, French			bravery and humanity	G, K
Willow, Herb	Rosebay		celibacy	Ho, O
Willow, Herb	Purple Loosestrife, Lythrum	*Epilobium* (Wa)	pretension	G, Ho, K, L, N, O
Willow, Weeping			mourning	Du, G, K, Le, N
Willow, Weeping	Willow of Babylon	*Salix babylonica* (Da, T)	melancholy	A, Da, Ho, L, O, T
Windflower, see Anemone				

FLOWER	OTHER COMMON NAME	BOTANICAL NAME	SENTIMENT	SOURCE
Winter Cherry	Ground Cherry,	*Physalis alkekengi* (Da, Wa)	deception	A, Da, G, Ho, K, O,
	Strawberry Tomato			Wa
Wintergreen, see Evergreen				
Wisteria			welcome, fair stranger	K
Witch Hazel		*Hamamelis virginiana* (Da, E, Ha)	spell, a spell, witchery	Da, E, G, Ha, Ho, K, O
Withered White Rose, see Rose				
Wolfsbane, see Monkshood				
Wood Sorrel, see Sorrel				
Woodbine, see Honeysuckle				
Woodruff			modest worth	N
Wormwood		*Artemisia* (Wa), *A. absinthium* (Da, T)	absence	A, Da, Du, G, Ho, K, L, Le, N, O, T, Wa
Wreath of Daisies, see Daisies				
Wreath of Roses, see Roses				
Xanthium, see Clotbur				
Xeranthemum, see Chrysanthemum, Eternal Flower				
Yarrow	Achillea Milfolia, Common Milfoil	*Achillea* (E), *A. millefolium* (Ha)	cure for heartache	E, Ha
Yarrow	Achillea Milfolia, Common Milfoil	*Achillea millefolium* (M)	thou alone canst cure	M
Yarrow	Achillea Milfolia, Common Milfoil	*Achillea millefolium* (Da, T, Wa)	war	A, Da, G, Ho, K, L, N, O, T, Wa
Yellow Acacia, see Acacia				
Yellow Auricula, see Auricula				
Yellow Balsam, see Balsam,				
Yellow Carnation/Pink, see Pink				
Yellow Day Lily, see Day Lily				
Yellow Gentian, see Gentian				
Yellow Iris, see Iris				
Yellow Jasmine, see Jasmine				
Yellow Lily, see Lily				
Yellow Marigold, see Marigold				
Yellow Narcissus, see Narcissus				
Yellow Rose/Sweetbriar, see Rose				
Yellow Tulip, see Tulip				
Yellow Violet, see Violet				
Yew		*Taxus* (Ha, M)	penitence	Ha, M
Yew		*Taxus* (Wa), *T. baccata* (Da)	sadness, sorrow	Da, Du, G, Ho, K, Le, N, O, T, Wa
Yoke Elm, see Elm				
York and Lancaster Rose, see Rose				
Yucca		*Yucca filamentosa* (Da)	authority	Da
Zea Mays, see Corn				
Zephyr Flower, see Anemone				
Zinnia		*Zinnia* (Wa), *Z. multiflora* (Ha, M, P)	absence	Ha, Ho, M, O, P, Wa
Zinnia		*Zinnia* (E)	I mourn your absence.	E
Zinnia		*Zinnia elegans* (Da)	thoughts of absent friends, thoughts of absence	Da, G, K, O

BIBLIOGRAPHY

Adams, John Stowell. *Flora's Album, Containing The Language of Flowers Poetically Expressed.* New York: Leavitt & Trow, 1848.

Bailey, Liberty Hyde. *The Standard Cyclopedia of Horticulture.* 3 vol. New York: Macmillan, 1937.

Bartram, William. *Travels through North & South Carolina, Georgia, East & West Florida 1791.* Reprinted as *Travels of William Bartram.* Edited by Mark Van Doren. 1928. Reprint. New York: Dover, 1955.

Bloom, Harold, ed. *Women Writers of Children's Literature.* Philadelphia: Chelsea House, 1998.

Burke, W. J. and Howe, Will D. *American Authors and Books 1640 – 1940.* New York: Gramercy, 1943.

Busch, Phyllis S. *Wildflowers and the Stories Behind Their Names.* New York: Scribner's, 1977.

Coats, Alice M. *The Treasury of Flowers:* London: Phaidon, 1975.

Coats, Peter. *Flowers in History.* New York: Viking, 1970.

Culpeper, Nicholas. *The English Physician.* London, 1652. Reprinted as *Culpeper's Complete Herbal & Physician.* Reprint of 1826 ed. Manchester, n.d.

The Bouquet: Containing the Poetry and Language of Flowers. By a Lady. Boston: Mussey, 1844.

The Box of Jewels. Hartford: Andrus, 1849.

Cupid's Basket: or the Language and Poetry of Flowers. New York: Leavitt, n.d.

Daniels, George. *The Floral Kingdom: Its History, Sentiment and Poetry.* Chicago: Standard-Columbian, 1891.

Dumont, Henrietta. *The Language of Flowers. The Floral Offering: A Token of Affection and Esteem; Comprising The Language and Poetry of Flowers.* Philadelphia: Bliss, 1864.

Edgarton, see Mayo, Sarah Carter Edgarton.

Elliott, Brent. "Say It with Flowers." *The Garden Journal of the Royal Horticultural Society.* 118: 371-73.

Esling, Catharine H. Waterman. *Flora's Lexicon: An Interpretation of The Language and Sentiment of Flowers.* Boston: Crosby & Ainsworth, 1865.

Ewan, Joseph and Nesta. *John Banister and his Natural History of Virginia, 1678-1692.* Urbana: University of Illinois Press, 1970.

Flowers, Their Language, Poetry, and Sentiment. Philadelphia: Porter & Coates, 1870.

Friend, Hilderic. *Flowers and Flower Lore.* 3rd ed. London: Sonnenschein, 1886.

Gerard, John. *The Herbal or General History of Plants.* London, 1597. Reprint of 1633 ed. New York: Dover, 1975.

Greenaway, Kate. *Language of Flowers.* London: Routledge, n.d.[1884].

Grieve, Maud. *A Modern Herbal.* 2 vol. Edited by Hilda Winifred Leyel. 1931. Reprint. New York: Dover, 1971.

Hale, Sarah Josepha. *Flora's Interpreter: or the American Book of Flowers and Sentiments.* Boston: Marsh, Capen & Lyon, 1832.
——. *Flora's Interpreter, and Fortuna Flora.* Rev. ed. Boston: Mussey, 1853.
——. *Flora's Interpreter, and Fortuna Flora.* 3rd rev. ed. Boston: Chase & Nichols, 1865.

Healey, B. J. *The Plant Hunters.* New York: Scribner's, 1975.

Hooper, Lucy. *The Lady's Book of Flowers and Poetry.* New York: Riker, 1851.

Hunt, John Dixon, ed. "Bartram's Garden Catalogue of North American Plants, 1783." *Journal of Garden History.* 16, January-March 1996.

Kirtland, C. M. [Caroline Matilda Kirkland]. *Poetry of the Flowers.* New York: Crowell, n.d.

The Language and Poetry of Flowers, and Poetic Handbook of Wedding Anniversary Pieces, Album Verses, and Valentines. New York: Hurst, n.d.

The Language and Poetry of Flowers with Floral Illuminations. London: Marcus Ward, 1875.

The Language of Flowers: An Alphabet of Floral Emblems. London: Nelson 1858.

[Shoberl, Frederick.] *The Language of Flowers; with Illustrative Poetry.* 5th ed. Philadelphia: Lea & Blanchard, 1839.

Latour, Charlotte de [pseud.]. *Le Langage des Fleurs.* 3rd ed. Paris: Audot, n.d.

Lehner, Ernst and Johanna. *Folklore and Symbolism of Flowers, Plants and Trees.* New York: Tudor, 1960.

Lincoln, see Phelps, Almira Lincoln.

Lindsay, T.S. *Plant Names.* London: Sheldon, 1923.

Mayo, Sarah Carter Edgarton. *The Flower Vase; Containing The Language of Flowers and Their Poetic Sentiments.* Lowell: Merrill & Heywood, 1848.

Neal, Bill. *Gardener's Latin.* Chapel Hill: Algonquin, 1992.

Okker, Patricia. *Our Sister Editors: Sarah Josepha Hale and the Tradition of Nineteenth-century American Women Editors.* Athens: University of Georgia Press, 1995.

Osgood, Frances Sargent. *The Poetry of Flowers and Flowers of Poetry.* Philadelphia: Lippincott, 1864.

Parkinson, John. *A Garden of Pleasant Flowers (Paradisi in Sole: Paradisus Terrestris).* 1629. Reprint. New York: Dover, 1976.

Phelps, Almira Lincoln. *Familiar Lectures on Botany,* 7th ed. New York: Huntington, 1838.

Pliny the Elder, Gaius Plinius Secundus. *Natural History. With an English Translation in Ten Volumes.* Cambridge: Harvard University Press, 1951.

Seaton, Beverly. *The Language of Flowers: A History.* Charlottesville: University Press of Virginia, 1995.

Smith, Isadore L. *A Gardener's Book of Plant Names.* New York: Harper & Row, 1963.

Taylor, John Ellor. *Flowers: Their Origin, Shapes, Perfumes, and Colours.* London: Hardwicke & Bogue, 1878.

Theophrastus. *Enquiry into Plants.* Translated by Sir Arthur Hort. Cambridge: Harvard University Press, 1916.

Todd, Pamela. *Forget-Me-Not: A Floral Treasury.* Boston: Little Brown, 1993.

Tyas, Robert. *The Language of Flowers; or, Floral Emblems of Thoughts, Feelings, and Sentiments.* London and New York: Routledge, n.d.

Waterman, see Esling, Catharine H. Waterman.

Warncliffe, Lord (James Archibald Stuart Mortley Mackensie). *The Letters and Works of Lady Mary Wortley Montagu.* Vol. I. Philadelphia: Carey, Lea & Blanchard, 1837.

Wells, Diana. *100 Flowers and How They Got Their Names.* Chapel Hill: Algonquin, 1997.

INDEX

*Entries in the Dictionary of the American Language of Flowers by Flower, pages 63-101, and in the appendix, pages 153-202, are listed alphabetically by flower and are not included in this index. Entries in the Dictionary of the American Language of Flowers by Sentiment, pages 105-141, are listed alphabetically by sentiment and likewise are not included in this index. Page numbers in **boldface** type refer to illustrations.*